Prisoners in the Bible

Prisoners in the Bible

ZACH SEWELL

WESTBOW
PRESS
A DIVISION OF THOMAS NELSON

WestBow Press books may be ordered through booksellers or by contacting:

WestBow Press
A Division of Thomas Nelson
1663 Liberty Drive
Bloomington, IN 47403
www.westbowpress.com
1-(866) 928-1240

ISBN: 978-1-4497-7975-7 (sc)
ISBN: 978-1-4497-7974-0 (e)
ISBN: 978-1-4497-7976-4 (hc)

Library of Congress Control Number: 2012923707

Printed in the United States of America

WestBow Press rev. date: 12/28/2012

For anyone whose life has been affected in some way by the painful reality of imprisonment.

Contents

Introduction

Prisoners in the Bible

I WAS RECENTLY LEADING A discussion with a small group of young adults at our church about the topic of *Prisoners in the Bible*. I asked them to participate in a word-association exercise. I brought up two words, *prisoner* and *Bible*, and asked them to respond with the first words or ideas that surfaced in their minds. We started with the word *prisoner* and the group's responses included: bondage, captive, hurtful, forgotten, Michael Vick, protection, conviction, unloved, cell, gang, *Shawshank Redemption*, bad, and criminal. We repeated the same exercise with the word *Bible* and the group responded with: God, memory-verses, boring, The Word, holy, love letter, wisdom, Leviticus, saved, Psalms, love, and joy.

What do prisoners have to do with the Bible? Is there any connection between the two lists of words above? What do the words *forgotten* and *captive* have to do with the words *joy* and *saved*? What does *conviction* have to do with *love*? What does *cell* have to do with *holy*? Although we oftentimes may not associate the two ideas, prison and prisoners are common themes in the Bible. Some parts of the Bible were written by a prisoner. We often overlook the fact that Jesus himself was arrested. This book will seek to explore the meaning and messages behind each prisoner's story in the Bible.

Jesus taught his followers that whenever they fed the hungry, gave water to the thirsty, provided a stranger with a place to sleep, gave clothes to those who needed them, cared for the sick, or visited people in prison, it was as if they were doing it for Jesus himself (Matthew 25:34-45). People sometimes assume that Jesus only spent time with seemingly perfect people. Jesus ministered to all people, "good" and "bad," and placed an emphasis on those who were not accepted in mainstream society: poor people, people with contagious skin diseases, foreigners, and other people that the world viewed as undesirable.

So what do the words *prisoner* and *Bible* have in common? A lot. Although the world tends to drift away from those with troubled situations and checkered pasts, Jesus tends to drift toward them. He was the only one touching the people with contagious skin diseases. This is great news for all of us because, regardless of where we are in life, we need the type of savior who will look past our brokenness and embrace us. Jesus is the intersection where the words *prisoner* and *Bible* meet. He binds words like *captive* and *saved* together. He represents the connection between *hurtful* and *love*, *forgotten* and *joy*, and *captive* and *saved*.

Each prisoner story in the Bible shares one element in common with the other prisoners in the Bible: God is at work in a unique way in their story. Regardless of whether the person had done good or bad, was guilty or innocent, or was treated fairly or unjustly, God still loved the person and wasn't finished with them despite the fact that they were in prison. God may work differently in one situation than in another, but that is part of His mysterious nature.

God is working in the lives of inmates today, just as He was thousands of years ago. God cares about every person's situation, and those who are incarcerated are no exception. People in prison today may at times feel alone and abandoned. Joseph had to have felt that way after his prison mate, who was supposed to help him once he was released, forgot all about him and went on with his life for two years before remembering him. God remembered Joseph, though, and was involved in his situation in the same way God knows every prisoner today and wants to be involved in each situation. God knows each person—even the ones that do not know him.

What is the Bible?

The Bible is a collection of separate books (some are actually letters) from many different writers that are all inspired by God. The stories and teachings shared in Scripture teach us about God and what it means to live a godly life.

If you think about it as a library, the Bible is broken up into two main sections: the Old Testament and New Testament. The Old Testament teaches about God's efforts to be in a relationship with His people before Jesus entered the scene. Its books consist of law, stories from history, poetry, and prophecy. The New Testament's books consist of stories about the life of Jesus, the spreading of His message, letters from leaders encouraging early Christian believers (some of these were written from prison), and one book describing an apocalyptic vision that God gave to His people.

Sometimes people see the Bible as a list of rules that tells us about all we have done wrong. It's sometimes represented that way. If you spend time reading it, though, you may find that the Bible has more to do with freedom than it has to do with rules. It is about second and third chances. It is the story of God seeking a relationship with us. It is not the story of some old man with a white beard reading a long list of rules in a monotone voice.

The Bible is a story of grace, mercy, and love. It is not about condemnation or making people feel guilty. Jesus said that he did not come into the world to condemn it, but to save it (John 3:17). The Bible has been misused as a guilt tool by some, but it is a story about God's love for every person and his sacrifice in order to be close with them. This excerpt from Psalm 107:10-16 is a good representation of God's compassion shown in Scripture:

> Some sat in darkness, in utter
>
> darkness, prisoners suffering in iron chains,
>
> because they rebelled against God's commands and despised the plans of the Most High.
>
> So he subjected them to bitter labor;
>
> they stumbled, and there was no one to help.
>
> Then they cried to the Lord in their trouble,
>
> and he saved them from their distress.
>
> He brought them out of darkness, the utter darkness, and broke away their chains.

Let them give thanks... for he breaks down gates of bronze and cuts through bars of iron.

God Works through the Imprisoned

Loneliness, disconnectedness, frustration, and loss of precious time in prison are nothing new to God. People have been bound by these elements for centuries. God has worked before in the lives of the imprisoned and will continue to do so. The idea that people in prison cannot have a significant impact on their world is contrary to what the Bible teaches. The apostle Paul wrote letters from prison that ended up being part of the Bible. When Joseph was released from prison, he helped save thousands of lives by helping people prepare for an upcoming food shortage. Most people who are in prison today will be released. To say that those people do not have a chance to make a significant contribution in God's service would be to go against what the Bible teaches.

Chapter One

Joseph:
The Difficulties of Prison Life

JOSEPH EXPERIENCED MANY OF THE toughest elements of incarceration. He had been betrayed. Those outside of prison discarded him. He was at times lonely, and probably sad. He was wrongly convicted of a sexual crime. He was misunderstood. His reputation was tied to a crime that he didn't commit.

Joseph's Early Life and Enslavement

The story of what led to Joseph's imprisonment began with his childhood. Joseph's brothers hated him because their dad loved him more than any of them. They sold him to a human trafficking group and told their dad that he had been killed. The traffickers sold him to Potiphar, an Egyptian government official who served as the captain of the guard. Joseph then worked in Potiphar's house. His hard work helped him earn Potiphar's trust. Potiphar gave him a promotion and made him a manager over all the workers in the house.

Potiphar's wife wanted to have an intimate relationship with Joseph. She was attracted to him because he was "handsome and well-built" (Genesis 39:6). The Bible says that she "spoke to him" each day, clearly in attempts to seduce him. She took offense when Joseph refused to sleep with her, and she reacted by accusing him of attempted rape, as we see in the following verses:

> One day he went into the house to attend to his duties, and none of the household servants was inside. She caught him by his cloak and said, "Come to bed with me!" But he left his cloak in her hand and ran out of the house.
>
> When she saw that he had left his cloak in her hand and had run out of the house, she called her household servant. "Look," she said to them, "this Hebrew has been brought to us to make sport of us! He came in here to sleep with me, but I screamed. When he heard me scream for help, he left his cloak beside me and ran out of the house."

—GENESIS 39:11-15

She kept his clothes with her and, until Potiphar got home, pretended to be traumatized. When he heard what had allegedly happened, he believed his wife and was steamed. The Bible says he "burned with anger" (Genesis 39:19). From his point of view, Joseph had trespassed into his marriage. Since Potiphar was the captain of the guard, he personally escorted Joseph to prison. That had to be a tense walk or ride—fueled by Potiphar's anger.

Potiphar probably gave Joseph a verbal beating on the way and maybe a real one when they got to the prison.

Joseph in Prison

So now everyone whom Joseph had ever known either thought he was dead or was a sexual offender. Even though he was innocent, he still had to live with the aching frustration of knowing that people believed he had sexually assaulted someone. Any reputation or friendship he had gained among the Egyptians was destroyed.

Joseph was held in a dungeon-like prison (40:15). As they are in many prisons today, the conditions there were uncomfortable. Psalm 105:18 describes Joseph's physical constraints: "They bruised his feet with shackles, his neck was put in irons." So not only did Joseph have to work through the emotional consequences of his imprisonment, but he also had to adjust to the physical discomfort as well.

After Joseph had been in for a while, someone new came to prison, whom Joseph hoped would be able to help him. The new prisoner was a man who had worked for Pharaoh, the ruler of Egypt. The man awoke from a strange dream and God gave Joseph the wisdom to interpret its meaning. The dream was a sign that the man would be released. Joseph asked him not to forget him once he was out:

> But when all goes well with you, remember me and
> show me kindness; mention me to Pharaoh and get
> me out of this prison. I was forcibly carried off from
> the land of the Hebrews, and even here I have done
> nothing to deserve being put in a dungeon.

> —GENESIS 40:14-15

The man most likely assured Joseph that he would try to help.

But the man "did not remember Joseph; he forgot him" (40:23). The word for *forgotten* in the original language used in the Bible can also mean that he *moved on*. It would have been hard for him to completely forget Joseph. He probably just forgot about the idea of helping him. In other places in the Old Testament, the same word used for *forgotten* can indicate "a slip from the memory or no one cares any longer to be involved with them."[1]

Since the man probably didn't have a real interest in helping Joseph, Joseph would have felt discarded. It can be tougher to be discarded than forgotten, because when someone discards us, we feel robbed of the natural need to matter to someone.

Joseph spent two more years in prison. I imagine those were hard, lonely years. In prison, it is comforting to receive letters, phone calls, and visits from friends and loved ones. Joseph had no one to write to or receive letters from. No visitors came to see him. The person who loved him most in the world, his father, thought he was dead (Genesis 37:33). He had no friends that we know of.

Joseph had lots of time to sit and ponder all that he had lost. Dietrich Bonhoeffer was a German pastor who became a prisoner during World War II because he opposed the Nazis. He wrote a poem in prison that probably reflects what Joseph felt, too:

> Stretched out upon my prison bed,
>
> I stare at the empty wall.
>
> Outside, a summer evening,
>
> regardless of me,
>
> goes singing into the country.[2]

In prison, it can feel as though the world is moving on without you. Joseph had to feel this way. There was no one who understood Joseph's situation, and no one he could confide in. He didn't know if his father thought he was dead or alive (he did not know what his brothers had told his father). What if his father had heard that he had assaulted Potiphar's wife?

In prison, all of the questions about one's future and life outside of prison can make uncertainty a present and unwelcome companion, especially if you don't have close friends to support you. The only things Joseph had were uncertainty and a dark, lifeless corner of a dungeon. But God had a plan for Joseph.

Joseph's Release from Prison

After two years had passed, Joseph's former prison mate finally saw some merit in mentioning Joseph to Pharaoh. The king had odd dreams that nobody else could interpret. This, of course, made the man recall his experience with Joseph.

The former inmate told Pharaoh about Joseph's God-given ability to interpret dreams. It's clear that the man felt bad about waiting two years before saying anything, because he started his address to Pharaoh by saying, "Today I am reminded of my shortcomings" (Genesis 41:9). The guards escorted Joseph from his cell and cleaned him up a little bit, probably so Pharaoh wouldn't be turned off by his grungy appearance. Then Joseph went before Pharaoh and interpreted his dreams. He told him that God was using the dreams to warn him about an upcoming food shortage crisis. Pharaoh released Joseph and put him in charge of preparing for the famine.

God's Ability to Use Suffering to Bring about Good

Joseph saved thousands of lives by storing up food. He even saved his brothers, who had betrayed him. Joseph told them that, through their evil actions, God had sent him ahead of them to save their lives as well as the lives of many others (Genesis 45:4-7). Joseph's story shows how God sometimes allows people to endure painful experiences when He can see a meaningful purpose behind the suffering (see John 9:1-7).

I know a couple in Florida whose son, Nathaniel, was born with multiple severe disabilities. During his life, he endured many surgeries and battled undiagnosed diseases. Sadly, he passed away when he was just four years old, which his mother describes as his "change of address," since he is in Heaven now. Nathaniel's life inspired his parents to help others who were facing challenges similar to the ones they had faced. They started an organization called *Nathaniel's Hope* which has helped churches across the United States start programs to help families with children who have special needs.

Like that family in Florida, Joseph was able to see the good that God could bring even in the midst of pain (Genesis 45:4-7). If you have an open heart, God may show you how He can take a bad situation in your life and use it to bring about good. Like Joseph, though, we may not be able to see the good for a long time. Helen Keller, who became blind and deaf before she was two, shared Joseph's attitude of embracing opportunities for good in the midst of pain:

> Although the world is full of suffering, it is also full
> of overcoming it. My optimism, then, does not rest
> on the absence of evil, but on a glad belief in the

preponderance of good and a willing effort always to cooperate with the good, that it may prevail.[3]

Keller's quote sheds light on key traits that we can learn from Joseph's life: patience in suffering and the acceptance and pursuit of the good that God may bring from it.

Points for Reflection/Discussion

Author's Note: *In these* Points for Reflection/Discussion *sections at the end of each chapter, there is space for you to write your responses if you would like to. If you would prefer to just think about the questions, then that's great too. You may also choose to write responses to some questions and reflect inwardly about others.*

➤ Who do you relate to most in Joseph's story? Joseph? His brothers? Potiphar's wife? Why?

➤ Read Genesis 45:4-8. Joseph had a positive view of what God was doing in his life. What is your view of God?

➤ No one came to visit Joseph or sent him letters. Who are you most thankful to have communication with?

➤ The Bible mentions twice that God was with Joseph while he was in prison (Genesis 39:21, 23.) Do you believe that God is with you?

➤ What experiences in Joseph's life (being betrayed, being tempted, gaining a bad reputation, being wrongly convicted, being lonely, being discarded) can you relate to most?

➤ God allowed Joseph to endure a lot of bad circumstances because he had a greater overall purpose for his life. In what ways may God use a difficult thing you are going through now for good in the future?

➤ Read John 9:1-7. What challenges did the man in the story face so that the work of God could be displayed in his life?

➤ When Joseph was released from prison, he did something meaningful. What are some goals, big or small, that you have for the time following your release? If you are not going to be released, what is something meaningful that you would like to accomplish from the inside of prison?

Chapter Two

How Joseph Handled Temptation

"Never let temptation become a conversation."
– Chris Seidman

IN THE LAST CHAPTER WE covered Joseph's story in a broad way. Now we'll look more closely at one of the episodes we mentioned in chapter one—when Potiphar's wife tried to seduce Joseph. We'll think about what lessons can be taken from Joseph's encounter with a tempting situation. One of the major differences we'll notice between Joseph's situation and our own is this: the strategies Joseph used to resist temptation that landed him in prison will, in most cases, help us avoid returning to prison.

It is important that we understand that temptation itself is not sinful. Jesus was tempted (see Matthew 4, Hebrews 4:15). What matters most is our response to temptation, and finding ways to avoid facing it. There are some lessons in Joseph's story that may help us deal with temptation effectively.

1st Piece of Joseph's Strategy: Don't be Caught Off-Guard

A friend of mine recently shared a good illustration from the world of video games about facing temptation. Most of us will remember the game *Super Mario*. It's about a plumber who faces all kinds of obstacles to rescue a princess who has been kidnapped by a dinosaur with a spiky shell. My friend's illustration about temptation had to do with the "ghost house" levels from the *Mario* game. In those levels, if you turned Mario's back on a ghost, the ghost would inch closer, but if you turned Mario's face toward the ghost, it would stop moving.

In the same way, when we turn a blind eye to temptation and are not prepared for it, it inches closer. Successfully dealing with temptation is like getting ready for an attack that you know is coming. We have to be prepared with a plan beforehand. If we are confronted by a tempting situation, we are more likely to give in if we are not ready with a defense. We have to be prepared for temptation that may show up in our lives, like Joseph was when his boss's wife tried to seduce him. When that happened, Joseph did not even consider following through with her proposition. He refused to sleep with her (Genesis 39:8), because he understood that doing so would have been immoral and ungodly (39:9).

2nd Piece of Joseph's Strategy: Be Aware of Your Godly Principles

Joseph had a clear understanding of his own godly convictions before his boss's wife tried to seduce him, and that helped him deal with temptation. If you read the story (Genesis 39:6-20), you'll notice that Joseph's responses to the temptation were immediate. He recognized that sleeping with his boss's wife was wrong as soon as she put the idea in his head. Because he was a godly person, he knew right away that the proposition was ungodly.

So what prepares *us* for temptation? We, like Joseph, need to know God. When do you feel closest to God? People relate to God in many different ways. Do you do things on a daily basis that make you feel close to God?

It's important to establish a daily connection with God. This happens through spiritual disciplines such as Scripture reading, prayer, service to others, and more. (See the *Daniel* chapter in this book for more on spiritual discipline.) If Joseph had not known God and had a clear understanding of his own principles that came from his relationship with God, he would have probably begun to justify the action in his mind, and that would have led to a bad decision.

3ʳᵈ *Piece of Joseph's Strategy:*
Don't Flirt With Tempting Ideas

Joseph made it a point to stay away from things that may have led him to sin. Genesis 39:10 explains that after the woman made her first attempt to seduce him, he refused to be around her. He was not going to "let temptation become a conversation." If we give thought to tempting ideas, they will gather momentum like a bicyclist going downhill with no brakes.

Let's face it. Sometimes we hang around places, people, or situations that we know are leading down a path to an immoral action—whether it's violence, sex, an act of revenge, gambling, or any crime. Joseph refused to be around a situation that could escalate into a mess. He wouldn't even be around his boss's wife, because he knew that if he let the temptation gain momentum, he might give in.

Likewise, when you first sense that a situation could lead to something wrong (even if it *feels* right or natural), that's when you should cut it out of your life. Don't flirt with the situation and see where it goes. When we do that, we start trying to justify indulgence. You can usually convince yourself that a certain action won't hurt if you spend enough time thinking about how it won't.

If someone is serious about a diet and has decided not to eat cookies, they shouldn't walk into a bakery right when the warm cookies are coming out of the oven just to admire the smell. You know the things that get you in trouble, and you will have an easier time dealing with them if you refuse to let ideas grow into possibilities.

I know a guy who has struggled with looking at pornography on the Internet, and wants to stop. He has decided to eliminate everything from his life that would make porn easily accessible. He even decided not to upgrade his cell phone to one of the newer models with video capability. He still has an older flip-phone that doesn't have access to the Internet. He takes the message of Jesus in Matthew 5:27-30 seriously.* He knows that

---

* It's important to understand that Jesus used hyperbole in this passage, which means that He purposefully used an exaggerated, unrealistic example to make a valid point, which was: take drastic measures to avoid situations that will cause you to sin. Following that teaching could mean moving or getting rid of a computer.

I knew of someone who actually harmed himself physically because of what Jesus said in this teaching. That is not what was intended.

if he eliminates sources that would cause temptation, he will be less likely to be tempted.

In his book, *Before Stones Become Bread: Becoming More Like Jesus by Resisting Temptation*, Chris Seidman provides this insight about temptation: "It starts with a suggestion and develops into a conversation within our minds."[1] If we let tempting ideas gain momentum, we will start trying to justify them. At a vulnerable moment, faulty reasoning will seem strong. If we decide beforehand the types of things we are not going to be involved in, we will do a better job of avoiding tempting situations entirely and have less vulnerable moments in which we have to make decisions.

By using Joseph's strategies of dealing with temptation, you may be able to greatly reduce your chances of returning to prison after you are released. In Joseph's story, he resists sexual sin, but through regular scripture reading you will learn what behaviors are and are not close to the heart of God (for example, see Galatians 5:16-26). Through scripture reading, you will be reminded of how to recognize temptation and be motivated to stay away from it.

It is important to remember, though, that nobody is perfect when it comes to temptation (except Jesus), and that we are saved by grace (Ephesians 2:8). It's okay to be disappointed when you succumb to temptation, but try not to let it depress you. Learn from it and pray for greater strength and insight to face it next time. I have heard football coaches talk about the importance of not letting one loss turn into multiple losses. In the same way, we should not let our guilt propel us into more sin.

Points for Reflection/Discussion

➢ What do we learn about sin from Romans 6:15-18?

➢ Jesus Himself suffered when He was tempted (Hebrews 2:18), but was successful in dealing with temptation. In what ways did Jesus deal with temptation in Matthew 4:1-11?

➢ Read Matthew 5:29-30. In that passage, Jesus uses hyperbole to teach about the importance of eliminating things from our life that cause us to sin. He did not literally mean for people to cut their hand off or gouge their own eye out. But He was telling his listeners to get rid of things in their lives that caused them to sin. What are elements of your life, either inside or outside of prison, that lead you into sin? How can you take steps to get rid of those things?

Chapter Three

Moses:
God's Ability to Use Anyone

IF YOU HAVE EVER FELT like you've had to look over your shoulder because of a warrant for your arrest, you may be surprised at what you have in common with one of the greatest leaders in the Bible. Moses, too, was at one time wanted by the authorities for a crime that he had committed.

Moses was not a prisoner, but he was on the run for (and guilty of) murder. His story shows the way that God is able to accomplish great things through anyone who is willing to serve Him—even people who have committed a crime as bad as murder. Forty years[1] after he committed murder, God used him to accomplish something significant. God chose Moses to lead his people out of slavery.

The Murder

Moses was a Hebrew born in Egypt during a time when Hebrew people were slaves there. At that time, Egyptians threw Hebrew baby boys into the Nile River because the government was concerned about the growing population of the Hebrews. Pharaoh's daughter saved Moses and he, a Hebrew, was raised in a royal Egyptian house.

The slaves in Egypt worked in abusive conditions (Exodus 1:12-14, 3:7). When Moses was a young man, he saw an Egyptian slave driver beating a Hebrew. If you have ever seen a defenseless person being abused, then you probably know the shock Moses felt. In a fight or flight moment, he chose to fight. His anger and adrenaline peaked in the same moment, which resulted in a life-changing decision. He looked around to see if anyone could see what he was about to do, and then he killed the Egyptian (Exodus 2:11-12).

Moses did not report the incident, but hid the body in the sand. Depending on how you look at it, this may seem like defense and not murder. It may even seem revolutionary. Regardless, in the culture that Moses lived in, just like most cultures today, the act was considered murder. Moses, with a clear motive, had killed a government employee and hidden the body.

On the Run

The next day, Moses found out that his secret *was not a secret.* He broke up a fight between two slaves and one of them said "Who made you ruler and judge over us? Do you want to kill me as you killed the Egyptian?" (Exodus 2:14). Have you ever had a moment when you learned that an action you thought was a secret was actually well-spread news? That's how Moses felt.

He was exposed. He knew the news would reach the Egyptians. Sure enough, Pharaoh heard about the killing and wanted Moses dead. He made it known that if Moses was found he would receive the death penalty.

Moses had to disappear. There was no time to gather any belongings. As long as he stayed in Egypt, he was in danger of death. He was like a mouse inside a snake's cage. So he fled the country immediately without a clear destination.

God's Call

Moses stopped running when he reached a land called Midian, which was outside of Egyptian domain and influence. He met and married a young woman there and worked as a shepherd for his father-in-law.

Forty years later, God spoke to Moses and told him that He wanted him to go back to Egypt. He wanted him to demand the release of the Hebrews from slavery, and lead them out of the country. Moses didn't think he was the person for the job. He resisted and said, "Oh, Lord, please send someone else to do it" (Exodus 4:13). He had other reasons for not wanting to go, but his personal history in Egypt played a role. He wouldn't want to go somewhere where he was known as a murderer and had a death warrant. God later assured Moses that all the people in Egypt who wanted to kill him were dead (Exodus 4:19).

The Way Our Past Equips Us

God chose Moses, with all of his baggage and fear, to be a leader. Moses may have seemed like a strange choice based on his history. But God didn't see it that way. Outside of Jesus, God never uses perfect people—because they don't exist. Everyone God used in the Bible had either a little hiccup or a major life event that they had to overcome and learn from in order to move forward and do what God wanted them to do. Moses was once known as a murderer, but he was remembered as the man God used to end the slavery of a nation. God even used Moses to teach others that murder is against God's commands (Exodus 20:13).

I recently heard a preacher say that with God's help, people can turn their stumbling blocks into stepping stones.[2] At one point in Moses' story, it looked like his mistakes were going to crush any hopes of a meaningful life he may have had. Later, God used Moses' history in Egypt to help slaves. God can use your history to help others, too. If you have committed a crime that hurt someone else, you may be in a good position to help prevent someone else from committing that same crime.

Recently, I saw a video testimony of a woman named Annie Lobert who was able to escape from a life of prostitution. In the video, she talked about her childhood and the unhealthy relationship she'd had with her father. She talked about the first time she sold herself and also described a time she was beaten by her pimp so badly that her nose and ribs were broken.

One night, after Annie had nearly overdosed on drugs, she called out to Jesus even though she wasn't even sure if He was real. After that, she learned to trust that through Jesus' healing she was whole, clean, and restored. She described the impact of her encounter with God:

> I knew God gave me a second chance. I got better and started reading my Bible...God just really started doing that inner-healing. The Holy Spirit was speaking to me telling me that I was beautiful, that I was chosen, that I was set apart, and sanctified and a holy vessel for Him.

I started to stand on Jesus' words: that I'm whole, that I'm healed, and I'm pure; that I'm a virgin in Him. And that gives me peace.

Annie later heard God's voice telling her to help others who were in a similar situation that she had been in:

The Lord said to me, "Annie I want you to go back to that strip. I want you to tell the girls that are in slavery that I love them." So that's what I'm called to do. To simply tell them: "God loves you. No matter where you've been, what you've done, no matter how dirty you feel. There's redemption. You are as white as snow—when you accept Him into your heart."[3]

God turned Annie's stumbling blocks into stepping stones. You may be a repeat offender who has been incarcerated multiple times. You may have come to terms with the fact that you've had your share of stumbling blocks and have a good understanding of what they are. If you are a committed follower of God, He can take what used to be your stumbling blocks and turn them into stepping stones. God may want you to become involved with a prison ministry and share your experience with younger people who are in prison for the first time. You could research a way to volunteer with a program that helps at-risk youth. They can benefit from your perspective.

Through spiritual growth and maturity, God can turn restrictions into avenues. God can use our past to equip us with compassion that we may not have had if it weren't for those events in our lives. We can't do it on our own. There were people Moses knew that God used to help him. When Moses voiced his hesitations about God's instruction for him to go to Egypt, God said, "*I will be with you*" (Exodus 3:12).

Points for Reflection/Discussion

➢ Read Exodus 2:11-15. Have you ever experienced a moment similar to Moses' when he knew his actions had been exposed?

➢ Later in his life, God used Moses as a great leader. Who looks to you as a leader or role model?

➢ At one time in his life, Moses was known as a murderer. But he was later remembered as someone who helped others. How do you want to be remembered?

➢ When you consider what God used Moses to do, what types of things do you think He could use you to do— big or small? Is there someone's life you could make a positive impact on?

➢ What is something God is doing in the world that you would like to be a part of?

Chapter Four

Samson:
Relationships and Influences

SAMSON, A MILITARY LEADER, HAD some unhealthy relationships that were detrimental to his livelihood. In the years following his wife's murder, he slept with prostitutes (Judges 16:1) and fell in love with a woman named Delilah who only wanted to use him.

Delilah pretended to love Samson but the only real interest she had in him was earning money by selling information to his enemies that would lead to his arrest. She took advantage of his weaknesses and sold information about his strengths. This led to Samson's imprisonment and a sentence of hard labor:

> Some time later, he fell in love with a woman in the
> Valley of Sorek whose name was Delilah. The rulers
> of the Philistines went to her and said, "See if you

can lure him into showing you the secret of his great strength and how we can overpower him so we may tie him up and subdue him. Each one of us will give you eleven hundred shekels of silver...."

Then the Philistines seized him, gouged out his eyes and took him down to Gaza. Binding him with bronze shackles, they set him to grinding grain in the prison.

—JUDGES 16:4-5; 21

Delilah pretended to be invested in a relationship that really meant nothing to her. Even though she repeatedly tried to hurt Samson, he stayed with her. It was as if he had tricked himself into thinking their relationship was just as meaningful to her as it was to him.

The Power of Relationships

Many of us have been involved in a relationship (and not always with a significant other) in which we are either influenced in a negative, ungodly way or influence others in an ungodly way. It's important to understand how our relationships affect us and how they affect others. This is especially important if you're trying to change your behavior or lifestyle. When someone is trying to stop smoking cigarettes, they know they can't stand around people who are smoking. They would be setting themselves up for failure. In the same way, we can't live godly lives by continuing to hang around people who cause us to do ungodly things.

There may someone, inside or outside of prison, who you need to sever ties with. Sometimes growing closer to God means we have to end relationships that pull us away from God. If there is someone who repeatedly influences you to do something you know God doesn't want you to do, then you should stop being around them even if that requires you to make a drastic change in your life.

I have a friend who was recently released from prison and decided to stay here in the Kansas City area instead of moving back to Wichita where he had lived before. It wasn't about the different cities; it was about the influences he knew in Wichita from before his incarceration. Even though he only knew a couple of people in Kansas City, he knew that if he went back to Wichita he would end up spending time with the same people he had before, which would cause him to relapse into his old behavior.

When I was a teenager, I used drugs.* When I quit, I had to make new friends and stop hanging around my old ones. I hesitated and wondered if I should keep hanging out with them in order to tell them about God and *why* I changed. That came later, and there is definitely a time for that. But the first thing I needed to do was mature as a Christian, and that meant being with mature Christians and learning from them. If you are trying to leave an old lifestyle, then you need to allow God to shape you into a mature Christian *before* you spend time with anyone who is involved with the lifestyle you just left.

Finding a Godly Mentor

It's important to be around people you look up to and to find a mentor who cares about you. Look for godly attributes in people that you could learn to imitate. Examples are an important part of everyone's lives. The New Testament contains several letters

---

* See the Gerasene Demoniac chapter for the full story.

that the apostle Paul wrote to different churches. In his letter from prison to the church in Philippi, Paul described two leaders, Timothy and Epaphroditus, that could serve as examples in his absence while he was imprisoned:

> I hope in the Lord Jesus to send Timothy to you soon, that I also may be cheered when I receive news about you. I have no one else like him, who takes a genuine interest in your welfare. For everyone looks out for their own interests, not those of Jesus Christ. But you know that Timothy has proved himself, because as a son with his father he has served with me in the work of the gospel. I hope, therefore, to send him as soon as I see how things go with me. And I am confident in the Lord that I myself will come soon.
>
> But I think it is also necessary to send back to you Epaphroditus, my brother, fellow worker and fellow soldier, who is also your messenger, whom you sent to take care of my needs. For he longs for all of you and is distressed because you heard he was ill. Indeed he was ill, and almost died. But God had mercy on him, and not on him only but also on me, to spare me sorrow upon sorrow. Therefore I am all the more eager to send him, so that when you see him again you may be glad and I may have less anxiety. Welcome him in the Lord with great joy, and honor people like him, because he almost died for the work of Christ, risking his life to make up for the help you could not give me.
>
> —PHILIPPIANS 2:19-30

What Christ-like attributes do you see in Paul's description of those two men? When you are released from prison, maybe you can make a point to be around people who have Christ-like attributes like Timothy and Epaphroditus had. Also, if you make it a point to develop Christ-like attributes in your own life, then people who look up to you will be encouraged by your example.

Conclusion

Samson could have surrounded himself with positive influences, but he was blinded by a relationship he thought would lead somewhere but only led to his incarceration. You do not have to continue in any relationship that you no longer feel is healthy for you. You are not a slave to any person, gang, or affiliation. If you are committed to Christ, your identity is in Him. Try to surround yourself with Christ-like influences.

Points for Reflection/Discussion

➢ Who are the biggest influences in your life?

➢ Read Judges 16:1-22. In what ways was Samson's relationship with Delilah not good for him?

➢ Is there a relationship that you have with someone that has only brought harm?

➢ Who do you relate to most in Samson's story? Samson or Delilah? Why?

➢ What Christ-like attributes did Timothy and Epaphroditus have?

➢ Who is someone that possesses Christ-like qualities that you would like to spend more time with?

➢ Read Philippians 3:17-4:1. What are the negative qualities of the first group Paul describes and the positive qualities of the second group?

➢ Samson was abused and sentenced to hard labor in prison (see Judges 16:21). Are you able to relate to that part of his experience?

Chapter Five

Manasseh:
Finding God in Prison

"Everyone deserves a second *second chance."*
—Michael Scott, *The Office*

MANASSEH'S STORY IS ONE OF someone who murdered his own children, but still experienced God's grace. He turned to God while he was in prison. He was into witchcraft and sorcery and the murders of his children were part of a sacrifice ritual to a god called Molech (Jeremiah 32:35). They took place in a valley outside of Jerusalem called Ben Hinnom (see sidebar on next page).

Manasseh as King

Manasseh was an influential person—an evil king of Judah. Although God gave him several chances to change his behavior, he wouldn't. He ignored God and kept persisting in evil. He fed on selfish sin. The list of immoral things Manasseh did is long (see 2 Chronicles 33:1-10 and 2 Kings 21:1-18).

Under Manasseh's leadership, Jerusalem became a breeding ground for crime and perversion. He led God's people into evil actions. The whole society followed Manasseh's example of ignoring God. God tried to speak to Manasseh, but instead of listening to God, Manasseh attempted to communicate with the dead through séances. He also "shed so much innocent blood that he filled Jerusalem from end to end" (2 Kings 21:16). He thought his own amusement was more important than other people's basic right to live.

Manasseh was later arrested by a foreign king, and it was in prison he finally looked for God:

> **Ben Hinnom**
>
> Child sacrifice to a god known as Molech (see Leviticus 18:21) became common in the valley of Ben Hinnom during the reign of evil kings like Hoshea, Ahaz, and Manasseh. Deuteronomy 18:9-12 associates this practice with dark magic.
>
> God spoke through the prophet Jeremiah about the valley of Ben Hinnom, saying: "They built high places for Baal in the valley of Ben Hinnom to sacrifice their sons and daughters to Molech, though I never commanded, nor did it enter my mind, that they should do such a thing..." (Jeremiah 32:35).
>
> Josiah, a good king, later destroyed a structure in the valley "so no one could use it to sacrifice his son or daughter" (2 Kings 23:10).
>
> In the New Testament, Jesus refers to Ben Hinnom (*Gehenna* in Greek) to draw a comparison to hell.

> The Lord spoke to Manasseh and his people, but they paid no attention. So the Lord brought against them the army commanders of the king of Assyria, who took Manasseh prisoner, put a hook in his nose, bound him

with bronze shackles and took him to Babylon. In his distress he sought the favor of the Lord his God and humbled himself greatly before the God of his fathers. And when he prayed to him, the Lord was moved by his entreaty and listened to his plea; so he brought him back to Jerusalem and to his kingdom. Then Manasseh knew that the Lord is God.

—2 CHRONICLES 33:10-13

Listening for God's Voice

There are three spiritual lessons we can take from Manasseh's story. First, we should listen closely for God's voice in our lives. Before he went to prison, Manasseh paid no attention when God spoke to him (2 Chronicles 33:10). He was preoccupied with immorality and ignored God's voice. Have you ever known God was speaking to you but you didn't listen? Maybe God has been trying to get your attention, but you have been putting him off.

There may be someone in your life God is using to speak to you. God may even be using prison to get your attention. He did that with Manasseh because He cared and had a bigger picture in mind for his life. Jesus said that He disciplines those He loves (Revelation 3:19).

Finding God in Prison

Second, Manasseh looked to God in his distress. He found redemption in prison. He reached out for God through prayer, and God listened. Even after he murdered his own children and others, after all the witchcraft, and after ignoring God, God still listened to his prayer. The most incredible thing about the holes we dig for ourselves by ignoring God is that we later find out that

God is there in the hole with us. He's willing to climb into our mess. We sometimes find God during our most broken moments because that's when we sincerely look for him.

Sometimes God has to change our perspective in order for us to be quiet and listen. Imprisonment was God's way of throwing cold water in Manasseh's face. He was humbled by the severity of his situation and looked to God for help. God saw more in Manasseh than a self-centered offender. God saw that he could be more than the scum of the earth.

God Hears Our Prayer

Third, God was moved by Manasseh's prayer. Sometimes we may not pray because we feel like God would never listen to us after all the things we've done to hurt other people. That's not the message of the Bible, though. God is compassionate.

If you have harmed others or influenced others to cause harm, God is still eager to be in a relationship with you. If your behavior has caused a ripple of damage, God still wants to bring good from your life. Manasseh had to deal with the practical and earthly consequences of his actions, and so do we. But if we earnestly seek God through prayer, He will provide the strength we need to endure the practical consequences of our actions.

God *was moved* by Manasseh's prayer. This shows the level of God's compassion and intimacy for people—even people who have done unspeakable things to others like murder. God was *moved*. What moves you? To illustrate the way that God was moved by Manasseh's prayer, I will share a few things that I have felt moved by, and you can think of things have moved you. I was *moved* the other day when I watched a video of dogs that had been neglected and abused. I feel *moved* when I hear about children in Africa who are forced to be soldiers or prostitutes. As a child I remember being *moved* when my oldest brother told me about an old guy at his work who was lonely and didn't really have any friends. What do you feel moved by? God is moved by *you*. He is moved by your prayer, just as he was by Manasseh's.

Grace and Compassion

There is no limit to the amount of grace God will give to someone who is truly repentant—even if they have messed up like Manasseh. Another person in the Bible who committed murder, King David, wrote this Psalm as a prayer about his actions:

> Have mercy on me, O God,
>
> according to your unfailing love;
>
> according to your great compassion
>
> blot out my transgressions.
>
> Wash away all my iniquity,
>
> and cleanse me from my sin.
>
> For I know my transgressions,
>
> and my sin is always before me.
>
> Against you, you only, have I sinned
>
> and done what is evil in your sight,
>
> so that you are proved right when you speak
>
> and justified when you judge.
>
> Surely I was sinful at birth,

sinful from the time my mother conceived me.

Surely you desire truth in the inner parts,

you teach me wisdom in the inmost place.

Cleanse me with hyssop, and I will be clean;

wash me, and I will be whiter than snow.

Let me hear joy and gladness;

let the bones you have crushed rejoice.

Hide your face from my sins

and blot out all my iniquity.

Create in me a pure heart, O God,

and renew a steadfast spirit within me.

Do not cast me from your presence

or take your Holy Spirit from me.

Restore to me the joy of your salvation

and grant me a willing spirit, to sustain me.

Then I will teach transgressors your ways,

and sinners will turn back to you.

Save me from bloodguilt, O God,

the God who saves me,

and my tongue will sing of your righteousness.

O, Lord, open my lips,

and my mouth will declare your praise.

You do not delight in sacrifice, or I would bring it;

you do not take pleasure in burnt offerings.

The sacrifices of God are a broken spirit;

a broken and contrite heart,

O God, you will not despise.

—PSALM 51:1-17

The message of Manasseh's story is not that your sins no longer matter. They do. The consequences and lingering pain, as you know, are real. They were for Manasseh and for David as well. God offers healing and grace in the midst of pain and consequences. His strength can sustain you.

Points for Reflection/Discussion

➤ Why do you think God was moved by Manasseh's prayer (2 Chronicles 33:10-13)?

➤ Sometimes God tries to speak to us and we don't listen. Do you ever feel that God has been trying to speak to you and you haven't been paying attention?

➤ Can you think of a time when you encountered God in a moment of brokenness like Manasseh did?

➤ Read Matthew 9:36, 14:14, and 20:34. In what ways is Jesus a person of compassion? How do 2 Corinthians 1:3 and James 5:11 describe God as compassionate?

➤ What parts of Psalm 51 stand out to you?

Chapter Six

Daniel:
Spiritual Discipline in Captivity

WHEN DANIEL WAS A YOUNG man, a foreign military invaded his home city. They burned all the buildings, killed many people without regard for age or gender (2 Chronicles 36:17), and in the aftermath of the attack, assaulted many women (Lamentations 5:11). The people of Jerusalem had no defense because most of their own military had fled. The survivors were chained up and forced to walk to a place called Babylon—leaving behind everything that was familiar to them. They became servants (2 Chronicles 36:20). It was a mass kidnapping.

Daniel was among those taken. When he arrived in Babylon, the government there changed his name to Belteshazzar, which was the name of a god that people in Babylon worshipped.[1] It was a way of mocking Daniel's commitment to the real God.

The book of Daniel was originally written for captives to

read for encouragement. People under foreign domination were in danger of compromising their beliefs by turning to idolatry. Daniel set an example by sticking to his core values in captivity.

Spiritual Growth in a Time of Captivity

Daniel did more than just stick to his beliefs during a time of disaster. He actually grew in his faith. In Babylon, he was challenged in ways he had never been before, and he made a habit of praying about new challenges. With each overwhelming problem he faced, Daniel depended more, not less, on God. A lot of people would have turned away from God if they had experienced what Daniel had. Many of the other captives probably did lose their faith in God. It would have been easy to after being kidnapped and seeing their friends killed.

Daniel was able to grow closer to God during a time of crisis because he was spiritually disciplined. Just as many other areas of life, such as diet, financial planning, and exercise, require discipline, so does a commitment to God. There's a difference between passively admiring God and purposefully seeking to develop a relationship with Him. There are many spiritual disciplines including prayer, fasting, service to others, humility, giving, hospitality, Bible study, and more. All of these things can strengthen our commitment to God.

Daniel understood that spiritual disciplines would help him endure his captivity in the healthiest way possible. He devoted himself to prayer. He made it a point to pray three times each day regardless of whether things were good or bad.

After Daniel and the other captives arrived in Babylon, the king instructed his officials to find young men from among the captive group who were dignified enough to serve in his palace.

Daniel stood out and was appointed to the king's service. He did well in his new position and the king promoted him above all the other officials.

The native officials didn't like the idea of a foreign slave outranking them. They looked for shady practices in his business, but couldn't find any, so they decided to murder him. They knew they couldn't get rid of him unless they found "something to do with the law of his God" (Daniel 6:5). They manipulated the king into making a new law that would, in effect, kill Daniel. For thirty days no one was allowed to pray to anyone except to King Darius. Non-compliance meant they would throw you into the lions' den to be eaten. The fact that the officials could count on Daniel to pray no matter what shows that they had taken notice of his genuine commitment to God.

When Daniel heard about the law, he "went home to his upstairs room where the windows opened toward Jerusalem. Three times a day he got down on his knees and prayed, giving thanks to his God, just as he had done before" (Daniel 6:10). Notice that his reaction came out of his already disciplined spiritual life. Prayer was a big part of who he had become. He didn't pray for the first time when trouble came—he prayed like he had before.

The Lions' Den

In his book, *Every Living Thing: Daily Use of Animals in Ancient Israel*, Obed Borowski points out that hunting lions was considered a "royal sport" (197) during biblical times. He explains how kings hunted lions for pleasure and thrill. The lions were often trapped and then kept in a park or were encaged and released when the king was ready to hunt. It's possible that the lions' den in Babylon that Daniel spent a night in was used to hold lions that a royal figure would later kill for sport. They, of course, also used the den as one of their unusual forms of capital punishment.

Ezekiel 19:7-9 uses the capturing of a lion by Babylonian people as imagery.

We sometimes treat God like a distant relative that we rarely talk to. We should want more out of our relationship with God than that. Prayer is not only about going to God when we need help. It's about gaining guidance and peace for whatever our everyday life involves. God should be more to you than a 911 call. Praying each day helps us develop a comfort level and confidence in God that we'll need when hard times do come.

A Christian who doesn't pray is like a bird that chooses to walk rather than fly. We always have the ability to pray, but we don't always take advantage of it. Daniel's confidence in God was high because he prayed every day. We tend to base our confidence in God on our circumstances. Daniel didn't. If he had, he would have stopped praying when he saw his neighbors of all ages killed in the streets of his home town and was then taken captive.

After the ban on prayer had gone into effect, the officials who were plotting to kill Daniel came into his house and found him praying. They informed King Darius, and Daniel was arrested and sentenced to die in the lions' den.

Trust Inside the Lions' Den

Daniel trusted in God, even in the face of death, and the Bible says that it was because of that trust that he was not physically harmed in the lions' den (Daniel 6:23). His devoted prayer life led to trust in God in the face of a life-threatening situation.

Daniel's confidence in God was high even when he was thrown into the lions' den. If we think of the lions' den as a metaphor for times of crisis in our own lives, we can see just how important trust in God can be. When we're in the lions' den, something is already wrong. Having faith in the lions' den is difficult because during the hardest times in life it can seem like God has already abandoned us. What role does God play in our life when lions are already surrounding us? What role does faith play when God has evidently not answered our prayers because we have already lost our job, we are being evicted from our house or sent to prison, or a loved one has just been diagnosed with a deadly disease? It's easier to question God when we're in the lions' den than it is to trust Him.

It is during threatening times that Daniel's example is the most powerful. He didn't stop praying when things went wrong for him—when he was taken as a prisoner of war to Babylon. We should not stop praying because of our own painful circumstances. Regular prayer leads to trust, peace, and confidence in God.

Climbing Out of the Lions' Den

When Daniel entered the lions' den, most people counted him out. Whether they liked Daniel or hated him, most people probably thought he would die in there. Daniel, however, surprised them by emerging from the lions' den unharmed. He survived because he trusted God (Daniel 6:23).

When you entered prison, people may have counted you out. People may not expect much from you once you leave prison. But with God's help, you can leave prison and make a positive impact on the world around you – even if nobody expects you to. That's what Daniel did (Daniel 6:25-28). When he climbed out of the lions' den, he fought against corruption and evil. What do you trust God will help you do when you leave prison?

Points for Reflection/Discussion

➢ How did consistent prayer affect Daniel's confidence in God even during tough times?

➢ Daniel's confidence in God was high because he prayed every day. Sometimes we base our confidence in God on our circumstances. When was a time in your life when your confidence in God was high? When was it low?

➢ In 2 Corinthians 12:7-10, the apostle Paul described a time when God didn't answer his prayer in the way he had hoped. Instead, Jesus told him "my grace is sufficient for you." Can you think of a time in your life when God did not say "yes" to your prayer but may have been trying to tell you "my grace is sufficient for you?"

Chapter Seven

Shadrach, Meshach, and Abednego:
Real Trust in God

WHEN THE BABYLONIAN FORCES INVADED Jerusalem and took Daniel and all of the other survivors of their attacks captive, the group of prisoners included three guys named Shadrach, Meshach, and Abednego. They, like Daniel, were forced to leave behind everything familiar in their lives and walk in chains to Babylon. Shadrach, Meshach, and Abednego weren't their real names. Those were new names that the people in Babylon assigned to them once they arrived. Their real names were Hananiah, Mishael, and Azariah. They lost a piece of their identity when they became prisoners.

The men's trust in God, though, helped them withstand troubles they would face during their captivity. The king in Babylon commanded all the people in Babylon, no matter what nation they came from or language they spoke, to worship an image of gold. The king threatened to kill anyone who didn't worship the image by throwing them in a furnace (Daniel 3:1-6).

Shadrach, Meshach, and Abednego refused to worship the image that Nebuchadnezzar had made. They were so serious about their commitment to God that they were willing to die for Him. When the king heard about this, he gave them a second chance:

> ... if you are ready to fall down and worship the image I made, very good. But if you do not worship it, you will be thrown immediately into a blazing furnace. Then what god will be able to rescue you from my hand?
>
> Shadrach, Meshach and Abednego replied to the king, "O Nebuchadenzzar, we do not need to defend ourselves before you in this matter. If we are thrown into the blazing furnace, the God we serve is able to save us from it, and he will rescue us from your hand, O king. But even if he does not, we want you to know, O king, that we will not serve your gods or worship the image of gold you have set up."

—DANIEL 3:15-18

The men chose to honor God even though there was a possibility that God wouldn't physically save them. The king was so mad that he turned the heat up on the furnace seven times its usual temperature. The heat killed the soldiers that took them up to the furnace, but it did not kill Shadrach, Meschach and Abednego. God intervened. Nebuchadnezzar was so astonished that he praised God for the way He had saved the three men (Daniel 3:28).

Practical Faith in God

For the three guys in this story, faith in God was not just a theory or a pattern of actions that made them good people. It was real. It was tangible. They depended on it. They were not sideline observers of God's work. They truly believed that the power of God would help them through their situation.

We, on the other hand, sometimes separate God from real life. C.S. Lewis described this by comparing our being to three concentric circles, each representing a realm of who we are. He said that the outermost part of our being is our *fantasy* realm, next is the *intellectual* realm, and in the middle is our *will*—the core of who we are. So, in his theory, you are represented by these three circles:

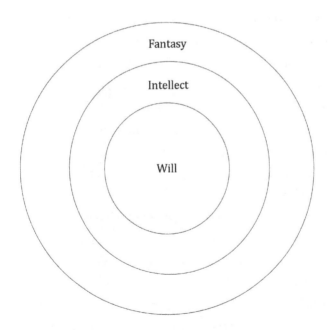

The *will* is what we actually do; it's the core of who we are. It's the reality. The *intellect* is made up of ideas we process and think about. The *fantasy* is what we imagine ourselves being. Lewis taught that Satan, whom the Bible describes as a deceiver, would want us to push everything having to do with God out of the *will* and into the *intellect* and *fantasy* realms of our being. That way we would merely *think* about God and about godly things like forgiveness, kindness, and helping others but not actually *act* on those things.[1] It would all be a fantasy.

Satan wants us to be surface-level Christians. But Shadrach, Meshach, and Abednego are examples of people who were committed to God at the deepest level of their being. They were not sideline observers of God who only watched. God factored into their everyday decisions, big and small.

Tim Allen (a former inmate himself who, depending on your age, is either the guy from *Home Improvement* or the voice of *Buzz Lightyear*) recently said, "On a philosophical level, I'm very religious. I call myself an intellectual Christian."[2] Allen's quote illustrates what C.S. Lewis was saying. People can be committed to God on an intellectual or philosophical level without being committed in their actions and lifestyle.

A few summers ago, I was a counselor at a children's camp. The camp staff was leading our group of kids through a high-ropes challenge course that consisted of several obstacles that required teamwork and courage to overcome. I was assisting at a station where the kids, secured to a rope, would climb up a pole about 25 feet high, stand on top of the pole, turn around, and then leap toward a trapeze bar hanging six feet away. If they didn't make it to the trapeze bar, they floated safely back down to the ground. Sounds easy, right? It looked easy enough to me. All afternoon I stood on the ground and coached the kids as they went through the steps of the station: "Okay, now just put your foot on top of the pole and step up. All right, now just keep your eyes on the trapeze bar and jump."

When our time at the ropes course was ending, the resident staff member said to me, "Hey, man, you haven't had a chance to do this yet." I said, "Oh, that's all right. It's about the kids, not us. We should probably be getting back to the campsite." I thought if I immediately spat out three readily-made excuses to a proposition, the guy would know I didn't want to do it. The campers heard the conversation, though, and insisted that I try. I smiled like it was no big deal. I put on the harness and climbed up the pole as if I was excited to get to the top. I reached the point where I was supposed to stand up on the top of the pole. I had been coaching kids to do it all day. I couldn't do it. I froze there for about five minutes with the kids staring at me. It was awkward. Somehow, I eventually stood up.

The next step was turning around to face the trapeze bar. The courage to do that took another five minutes to show up. Next, of course, was the jumping part. It was one of those situations in which everyone keeps counting to three with anticipation, but you never do the thing they're anticipating. Finally, I ~~jumped~~ stepped off of the pole and floated slowly back down. One counselor told me my "jump" looked less like a jump and more like I had been hit with a purse.

Trust in God can be like that ropes course exercise. It's easy to imagine ourselves doing it, but it can be tough to put into practice. Trust is especially difficult when we're faced with a situation when we have to rely on God like we haven't before. Shadrach, Meshach, and Abednego had confidence that God would do what was best and trusted Him in their situation.

Points for Reflection/Discussion

➤ Read Psalm 114:3-8. How do idols like the one Nebuchadnezzar made compare to the real God? How do things we put before God compare to Him?

➤ Who is someone you know who has Christ at the center of their life? What qualities do you admire about them?

➤ When was a time when you truly had to rely on God?

➤ Proverbs 3:5-6 says, "Trust in the Lord with all your heart and lean not on your own understanding; in all of your ways acknowledge him, and he will make your paths straight." What is appealing to you about that promise?

➤ Read Isaiah 42:16. In what ways does God promise to lead people even during difficult times and in unfamiliar places?

➤ Read Matthew 6:33. What does this verse teach about making God a priority?

Chapter Eight

Jeremiah:
Fear in Prison

JEREMIAH'S STORY WILL RESONATE WITH those who sit tucked away in an uncomfortable corner of an unhappy prison. It will resonate with any inmate who has been on the receiving end of aggression in the form of abuse. It's the story of someone who understands how solitary confinement and the neglect of basic needs can affect one's health and psyche. It's the story of someone who feared for his life in prison.

Jeremiah was one of God's prophets, which means he boldly shared messages of God. A man named Irijah, who was the captain of the guard for a prison, held a grudge against Jeremiah for speaking out against Irijah's grandfather (see Jeremiah 28). Irijah arrested Jeremiah on fabricated charges and sent him to prison as an act of retaliation. Jeremiah wasn't safe in the prison:

...he (Irijah) arrested Jeremiah and brought him to the officials. They were angry with Jeremiah and had him beaten and imprisoned in the house of Jonathan the secretary, which they had made into a prison.

Jeremiah was put into a vaulted cell in the dungeon, where he remained for a long time. Then King Zedekiah sent for him.... Jeremiah said.... "But now, my lord the king, please listen. Let me bring my petition before you: Do not send me back to the house of Jonathan the secretary, or I will die there."

—JEREMIAH 37:14-17, 20

Abuse and Solitary Confinement

Jeremiah's experience in prison was a painful one. His time there was filled with abuse, danger, and possibly neglect. He feared for his physical well-being, and for good reason. He had been beaten by the people running the prison on his first day there, and the captain of the guard held a grudge against him.

The prison environment alone was enough to cause depression and disorientation—he was in a dungeon, in solitary confinement in a vaulted cell. It would have had little—if any—light, and poor airflow and no air circulation. No wind gusts could have reached his vaulted cell in the basement of the prison. He had only thick, stuffy air. He was there for a long time and may not have had any good indication of how much time had passed. Weeks probably seemed like months, and he probably felt a lifetime's worth of sorrow in one year. King Zedekiah later ordered that Jeremiah be taken to a different prison and specifically ordered that a regular eating schedule be prearranged for him (Jeremiah 37:21), which could indicate that his basic needs had been neglected in the dungeon.

All of the hazards that came with Jeremiah's incarceration, if added up, had to be a major threat to his psychological health. It was stuffy, scary, and disgusting. His well-being was threatened by the environment of the prison and by those in charge of it. It was uncomfortable. It was a lonely place where the only thing that filled the emptiness was the stuffy air and threat of abuse. And it all lasted a long time.

Fear

Fear lives in every prison. It hovers in the air of the unknown and all too familiar. It's an allergy that peaks year round. God addresses fear all throughout the Bible. I recently heard a preacher say that there is a teaching in Scripture on fear for every day of the year. I believe it. God is sympathetic toward the fearful and wants to encourage them (see Isaiah 35:3-4). If you are afraid, God understands.

In the Bible, fear is usually represented as an obstacle to be overcome, but it can be a healthy instinct if it's not overdeveloped. Jeremiah acknowledged his fear and it improved his prison situation (Jeremiah 37:20). Fear as a survival instinct is helpful, but fear as a lens through which we see the world is burdensome. God is the one who can help you manage fear.

God's Ability to Comfort

God can comfort people in bad situations. One way we can connect with God is through prayer. A decoration hanging in my friend's kitchen simply says *Prayer Changes Things*. It's true. Jesus teaches us to be bold and persistent when we pray (see

Luke 11:5-13). If you are concerned about your physical well-being in prison, you should be praying more than usual and not less. Ask others to pray for you, too. Don't give up if you aren't immediately able to see a response from God.

Below are a handful of passages from the Bible that teach about God's power to comfort through His presence and by answering prayer. It may be helpful for you to read them often and even memorize them. When we memorize Scriptures, they're more likely to come to mind when we need them the most. Even if you are not in physical danger but you feel anxious about something, these passages can offer encouragement:

> I sought the Lord, and he answered me;
>
> he delivered me from all my fears.
>
> Those who look to him are radiant;
>
> their faces are never covered with shame.
>
> This poor man called, and the Lord heard him;
>
> he saved him out of all his troubles.
>
> The angel of the Lord encamps around those who fear him,
>
> and he delivers them.
>
> —PSALM 34:4-7

> My help comes from the Lord,
>
> the Maker of heaven and earth.
>
> He will not let your foot slip—
>
> he who watches over you will not slumber;

...

the Lord will watch over your coming and going

both now and forevermore.

—PSALM 121:2-3, 8

O Lord, you have searched me

and you know me.

You know when I sit and when I rise;

you perceive my thoughts from afar.

You discern my going out and my lying down;

you are familiar with all my ways.

Where can I go from your Spirit?

Where can I flee from your presence?

If I go up to the heavens, you are there;

if I make my bed in the depths, you are there.

If I rise on the wings of the dawn,

if I settle on the far side of the sea,

even there your hand will guide me,

your right hand will hold me fast.

—PSALM 139:1-3, 7-10

I will lead the blind by ways they have not known,

along unfamiliar paths I will guide them;

I will turn the darkness into light before them

and make the rough places smooth.

These are the things I will do;

I will not forsake them.

—Isaiah 42:16

The Lord himself goes before you and will be with you; he will never leave you nor forsake you. Do not be afraid; do not be discouraged.

—Deuteronomy 31:8

For I am convinced that neither death nor life, neither angels nor demons, neither the present nor the future, nor any powers, neither height nor depth, nor anything else in all creation, will be able to separate us from the love of God that is in Christ Jesus our Lord.

—Romans 8:38-39

Points for Reflection/Discussion

➤ What part of Jeremiah's experience are you most able to relate to?

➤ Have you ever been fearful for your well-being like Jeremiah was?

➤ When have you prayed about a situation and it improved?

➤ Which of the above passages is the most comforting to you?

Chapter Nine

Hagar:
Restraining Order

HAGAR WAS AN AFRICAN WOMAN who became part of a Hebrew family as a slave, was sexually exploited, and was then kicked out of the family's community and given a restraining order so she could not return.

Hagar was born in Egypt, but when she was a young woman she was given as a slave by an Egyptian ruler to Abraham and Sarah, a Hebrew couple that was visiting Egypt at the time. The ruler gave them several cattle and servants (Genesis 12:16), and Hagar was among those servants. So Hagar, having no choice, left Egypt with the couple and spent years traveling with them. She became a maidservant to Sarah.

Sexually Exploited

Sarah and Abraham were unable to have children for many

years. God had promised Abraham that he would have many children, but Sarah didn't believe that she could be the one who would give birth to Abraham's children. She told Abraham to sleep with Hagar, and said, "Perhaps I can build a family through her" (Genesis 16:2). Sarah wanted Hagar to have a child that Sarah could claim as her own.

Hagar slept with Abraham and became pregnant. It may have been an ongoing sexual encounter between the two—until Hagar conceived. When she realized she was pregnant, Hagar "despised" Sarah (Gen 16:4). She was already a slave, so her life was hard enough, but it became even worse when she had to have sex with her owner and have a child that wouldn't even be considered her own.

It would seem like Sarah was abusing Hagar's personal rights to fulfill her own intimate wishes, but it's clear that Hagar didn't have any personal rights. Hagar was being used as a means to an end. Her body was someone else's property, and her child was going to be as well.

Hagar's Restraining Order

Years later, Sarah was able to become pregnant by Abraham and had her own child. When her son was born, she wanted to forget that she had ever asked her husband to have a child through another woman: "and she said to Abraham, 'Get rid of that slave woman and her son, for that slave woman's son will never share in the inheritance with my son Issac'" (Genesis 21:10). At one point, Sarah had wanted to build her own family through Hagar. When she didn't need Hagar anymore, she wanted her and her son gone. People like to move on from their mistakes, but this seems to be Sarah's way of trying to pretend hers never happened. She got rid of them like they were old pieces of furniture that didn't match the new household décor.

Hagar was not even given a full day to process the major life change she was about to experience. The only courtesy Abraham gave Hagar after Sarah told him to get rid of her and her son was to wait until morning and not send them out in the middle of the night. Abraham sent Hagar and her son away with only as much food and water as Hagar could carry on her shoulders (Genesis 21:14). They weren't allowed to go back.

We could read this story and think that being kicked out was good news for Hagar, since she was being set free. But she had never had to live or travel on her own before. Since her son had been alive, she had never had to worry about food or water for him. She had never been independent, and didn't live in a culture in which a woman in her circumstance—a single, foreign mother and former slave—could just start over. She was separated from all the resources and people she had known for years.

In just one day, Hagar's circumstances quickly became desperate due to a lack of food and water. But God provided water and encouragement when they were near death. God watched over Hagar and her son, and he later married a woman from his mother's home country: "God was with the boy as he grew up. He lived in the desert and became an archer. While he was living in the Desert of Paran, his mother got a wife for him from Egypt" (Genesis 21: 21).

God Sees You

Hagar once described God by saying, "You are the God who sees me" (Genesis 16:13). This was when she was pregnant with Abraham's child. She had run away from Abraham and Sarah, and God sent an angel to comfort her (Genesis 16:7-13). Since she was from Africa and had lived as a slave for Hebrew people, she had probably heard multiple teachings about God. But her clearest understanding of God came by personally experiencing His compassion. She knew that He had seen her during her difficult situation. She knew that He had heard her cries. She knew that even though her life was hard, God understood. She named her child *Ishmael*, which meant *God Hears*.

You may feel like you can relate to Hagar. You may know what it's like to be used as a means to an end. Maybe you had a wanted or unwanted series of sexual encounters, but you felt abandoned afterward. Maybe someone promised to help you raise a child, but they didn't follow through on their commitment. Maybe you've been sexually exploited for someone else's gain. Maybe someone who never really loved you took advantage of you sexually. Maybe someone impregnated you but wants nothing to do with you or your child. The message of Hagar's story is that God sees you and loves you. God sees the pain that is brought about by abuse, neglect, rape, and abandonment.

God understands your life. God is not like someone who sees another person and makes a quick judgment about them without knowing their story. He understands. If you have been sexually promiscuous, God understands your story and wants to help you live a new life.

Points for Reflection/Discussion

➤ Hagar described God as "The God who sees me" (Genesis 16:13) based on her personal experience with Him. Have you ever experienced God's presence during a difficult time?

➤ Have you ever been used like Hagar?

➤ Read John 4:1-26; 39-42 and John 8:1-11. How does Jesus help both of these women who had been sexually promiscuous?

➤ If you have been used sexually in the past, what steps can you take to assure that you will not be in the future? What relationships will need to end? It may be helpful to journal about what you envision a healthy relationship with the opposite sex to be like and spend time praying that God will provide that for you.

➤ To whom in the story of Hagar, Ishmael, Abraham, and Sarah do you relate to the most?

Chapter Ten

John the Baptist:
Murdered in Prison

JOHN THE BAPTIST WAS PASSIONATE about God and about what God was doing through his cousin and friend, Jesus. John wasn't afraid of confrontation and his boldness offended some influential people who had the power to hurt him. As a result, he went to prison.

John told the governor of the area, Herod Antipas, that it was wrong for him to have a relationship with and be married to his brother's former wife, Herodias. She was seeking more power than her previous husband, Herod-Phillip, was able to give. So she left him for Herod Antipas. Herodias was so bothered by what John said that she "nursed a grudge against John and wanted to kill him" (Mark 6:19). So Herod had John arrested and put in prison.

Herod Antipas came from a family known for violence and murder. His father, Herod the Great, was an insecure and blood-thirsty leader who executed anyone who threatened him, including his three oldest sons.[1] When Jesus was born, Herod the Great wanted to kill Him. Jesus' parents, Joseph and Mary, were able to leave the area with Jesus. When Herod couldn't find Jesus, he ordered that all the boys in Bethlehem two years old or younger be killed. Herod Antipas, who imprisoned John, had absorbed his father's immoral characteristics (Luke 3:19-20).

Herod did not want John to die, though, and protected him from his wife. John and Herod apparently formed a meaningful relationship while Herod kept John in prison. Mark 6:20 says that Herodias, the woman, was not able to kill John "because Herod feared John and protected him, knowing him to be a righteous and holy man. When Herod heard John, he was greatly puzzled, yet he liked to listen to him." So there was obviously some type of a mentoring connection between the two men.

Herod's acquaintance with John may have been the most meaningful relationship he ever had. Even though Herod had done a lot of things to hurt other people, John didn't think it was a waste of time to visit with him. John saw something in Herod worth investing in. John was probably the only voice of God in Herod's life and was probably the only person bold enough to be honest with him.

John's Execution

Herod's birthday came and Herod threw a banquet and invited his high-ranking officials, military commanders, and some leaders in the community.

During the party, probably after there had been a good amount of drinking, Herodias's daughter (who if we're keeping track was Herod's niece *and* stepdaughter) danced, probably provocatively, for Herod and his guests. Everyone liked the girl's performance so much that Herod spoke up and promised to grant any request she could think of. He probably did this to impress his guests and remind them of how powerful he was. She went and chatted with her mother, Herodias, and came back with a firm decision: "I want you to give me right now the head of John the Baptist on a platter" (Mark 6:25).

The girl's demand made Herod stressed and flustered. He didn't want to kill John, but he also didn't want to go back on his word in front of all his important colleagues and military officials at the party. He had a reputation of being harsh, so if he explained to everyone that he didn't want to kill John because he respected him and he was interesting to talk with, then they would think that Herod was a softy. Folding under social pressure, he sent an executioner to John's cell. The executioner killed John, and John's head was presented on a platter later at the party.

Knowingly Disobeying God

Sometimes we know that what we're doing, even as it's happening, goes against how God wants us to act. That's how Herod must have felt when he ordered John's execution. John had been the only godly person that took time to talk with Herod. A writer named Oswald Chambers said that by killing John, Herod "silenced the voice of God in his life."[2] When we knowingly do what we know we shouldn't, we push ourselves away from God. We silence His voice in our life.

God's Heart for All People

John cared enough about someone like Herod Antipas,

who was known for evil and would later kill him, to develop a relationship with him. When John saw people like Herod, he didn't see a lost cause. He saw someone worth investing in and teaching even while he was locked up at Herod's command.

That John spent time talking with Herod shows his understanding of the heart of God. He understood that people could change with God's help. God desires redemption for all people, even people with bad reputations. God wants people who have pushed Him away to look for Him again.

A Question for Jesus from Prison

Before his imprisonment, John was confident and bold about his belief that Jesus was the Son of God. While he was in prison, though, John sent two of his students who had visited him to Jesus to ask, "Are you the one who was to come, or should we expect someone else?" Jesus responds by performing miracles in the sight of John's students and telling them to:

> Go back and report to John what you have seen and heard: The blind receive sight, the lame walk, those who have leprosy are cured, the deaf hear, the dead are raised and the good news is preached to the poor. Blessed is the man who does not fall away on account of me"
>
> —LUKE 7:22-23

It's okay to have questions for or about God while you're in prison. John received an answer to his question about Jesus. Since he was in prison, John couldn't see for himself what Jesus was doing. Tough questions for God are natural even for people who have a deep faith, like John did. In prison, we can doubt things we were once certain of. Like John, we may want to ask God, "Are you really who I think you are?" It is better to ask tough questions of God than to abandon your faith altogether. We can listen for God's answer by being spiritually disciplined through prayer, silence, and Bible study.

Points for Reflection/Discussion

➤ In what ways have you pushed God away in the past?

➤ John was passionate about God's truth and shared his beliefs with boldness. Do you believe in God strongly enough to share about Him with other people?

➤ John was a mentor to Herod while Herod kept him in prison (Mark 6:20). He taught Herod, and Herod considered him to be a holy person. Who is someone in your life that is a mentor to you? Does anyone look to you as a mentor?

➤ John's death affected a lot of people, including Jesus. When Jesus heard about what had happened, "he withdrew by boat privately to a solitary place" (Matthew 14:13). If you have lost a loved one, is it comforting to know that Jesus also experienced the grief of losing a friend to death?

➤ John was a selfless person who understood his purpose of pointing others toward Jesus. In fact, many artists who have painted John the Baptist show him pointing away from himself and to God. In his life, John was like a sign pointing others to Jesus. Read John 1:21-26. It's clear that John understood his purpose and didn't claim to be something he wasn't. What purpose do you feel God has for your life?

➢ For more on John the Baptist, read Matthew 3; 11:1-18; 14:1-21; Mark 1:1-8; 6:14-29; Luke 1:5-80; 3:1-20; 7:18-28; John 1:1-42; and 3:22-26. What new things do you learn in these passages about John that you admire? What do you learn about Jesus from John's teaching?

Chapter Eleven

The Gerasene Demoniac:
God's Power to Change a Life

IT'S EASY TO THINK THAT some people, based on their behavior, are beyond helping. There are people who have had their chances to do well and have blown it. People who seem like they'll never change. People who don't seem to be led by any conscience of good will. People who will never contribute anything meaningful to society.

There is a man in the Bible who seemed like he could never change, but did. He was possessed by multiple demonic spirits, lived in the tombs, cut himself with stones, attacked people, and never wore clothes. The New Testament writer Mark describes the man's desperate circumstance before he met Jesus:

> When Jesus got out of the boat, a man with an evil
> spirit came from the tombs to meet him. This man

lived in the tombs, and no one could bind him any more, not even with a chain. For he had often been chained hand and foot, but he tore the chains apart and broke the irons on his feet. No one was strong enough to subdue him. Night and day among the tombs and in the hills he would cry out and cut himself with stones.

—MARK 5:2-5

Three writers in the Bible tell the story of the Gerasene demoniac, and each account sheds unique light on his situation. Since we learn so much about this man from three different sources in the Bible, a chart may be helpful to organize the information:

The Person/ Threat to the Person	Threat to the Public	The Village's Response
MARK: "A man with an evil spirit ... lived in the tombs, and no one could bind him any more, not even with a chain. For he had often been chained hand and foot, but he tore the chains apart and broke the irons on his feet. No one was strong enough to subdue him. Night and day among the tombs and in the hills he would cry out and cut himself with stones" (5:2-5).	Psychological threat of constantly hearing the man cry out from the hills and in the tombs during the night and day Concern of the public (including children) witnessing the act of or results of self-mutilation Could not be detained Phenomenal strength	Unsuccessful detainment through chains on his hands and irons on his feet Repeated attempts to subdue him Failure to physically overpower him

MATTHEW: "Two demon-possessed men coming from the tombs.... They had become so exceedingly violent that no one could pass that way" (8:28).	Excessive violence Threat of attack which kept people from taking certain paths near the tombs	Avoiding certain areas Fear/effect on the general morale
LUKE: "He was from the town. For a long time this man had not worn clothes or lived in a house, but had lived in the tombs.... Many times [the spirit] had seized him, and though he was chained hand and foot and kept under guard, he had broken his chains and had been driven by the demon into solitary places" (8:27-29).	The psychological impact on the town of knowing the man before he was possessed and then seeing him become possessed Indecent exposure which would have displayed marks of self-mutilation	Chained him hand and foot Tried to keep him under guard, but he escaped into the hills and tombs

Demon Possession

This story may seem pretty crazy. The writer assumes the reader has thought about demon possession before. So how did someone or how does someone become possessed by an evil spirit? The Gerasene demoniac was probably involved in a practice in which he engaged dark powers, whether in a pagan temple or at a séance in someone's house. People have a fascination with things like magic, but the Bible teaches us to have nothing to do with it. Deuteronomy 18:10-11 says: "Let no one be found among you who sacrifices his son or daughter in the fire, who practices divination or sorcery, interprets omens, engages in witchcraft, or casts spells, or who is a medium or spiritist or who consults the dead."

The man may have been seeking to leverage his own power by becoming stronger through unseen forces. In the Gerasene culture he grew up in, there were no Scriptures like Deuteronomy that warned people to stay away from magic. He may have invited the dark spirits into his body, thinking they would give him power that would impress others or maybe even make him rich. That may seem illogical, but there is a story in the Bible about a slave girl who told people's fortunes through the power of an evil spirit. People paid her owners for fortunetelling (Acts 16:16-18).

Somehow, the Gerasene man entered into a relationship with Satan in which body, soul, and spirit were meshed. He became possessed by a large group of evil spirits that completely controlled his life and actions. Whatever he did to engage the spirits, it backfired and made his life the closest thing to a literal hell on earth that anyone has ever experienced.

One of my college professors served as a Christian missionary for 26 years in Ghana, West Africa. While there, he encountered people who had engaged satanic forces. He described situations in which a person would become demon-possessed because they first opened a figurative door, attempting to leverage dark power in their favor. He told me, "The primary motive in manipulation of such powers is self-promotion. We have seen many instances in which people attempted to use spiritual forces to inflict harm on someone else only to have those powers come back on themselves. This is very, very, common."

The Effect of the Man's Behavior on Others

As is oftentimes the case, the man's behavior affected

more people than just himself. When people are in trouble, the consequences of their behavior hurt people who love them. The Gerasene demoniac's "personal" problems affected a whole community. He had become excessively violent (Matthew 8:28)*, so the villagers tried to keep him in chains and under guard (Luke 8:29). People avoided the tombs because of him.

The demoniac probably attacked several people. The original language of Matthew's account of the story says that the man had become *exceedingly* violent, indicating a series of attacks that had become progressively more severe. How badly the victims were hurt is unknown. There are other instances in the Bible in which a demon-possessed person hurt others. In Acts 19:13-16, a group of men attempted to force a demon out of a man and "the man who had the evil spirit jumped on them and overpowered them all. He gave them such a beating that they ran out of the house naked and bleeding."

The Man's Encounter with Jesus

Let's take a moment to read what Mark shares about the man's encounter with Jesus. I think it's best to picture this whole scene as if you were seeing it on the big screen in a movie theater, with the camera switching between all the different perspectives as it happens:

> When he saw Jesus at a distance, he ran and fell on his knees in front of him. He shouted at the top of his voice, "What do you want with me, Jesus, Son of the Most High God? Swear to God that you won't torture me!" For Jesus had said to him, "Come out of this man, you evil spirit!"

---

* Matthew's account of the story describes two men that were possessed by multiple demons. Mark and Luke each describe just one man.

Then Jesus asked him, "What is your name?"

"My name is Legion," he replied, "for we are many."
And he begged Jesus again and again not to send them
out of the area.

A large herd of pigs was feeding on a nearby hillside.
The demons begged Jesus, "Send us among the pigs;
allow us to go into them." He gave them permission,
and the evil spirits came out and went into the pigs.
The herd, about two thousand in number, rushed down
the steep bank into the lake and were drowned.

Those tending the pigs ran off and reported this in the
town and countryside, and the people went out to see
what had happened. When they came to Jesus, they
saw the man who had been possessed by the legion of
demons, sitting there, dressed and in his right mind;
and they were afraid. Those who had seen it told the
people what had happened to the demon-possessed
man—and told about the pigs as well. Then the people
began to plead with Jesus to leave their region.
As Jesus was getting into the boat, the man who had
been demon-possessed begged to go with him. Jesus
did not let him, but said, "Go home to your family and
tell them how much Jesus has done for you, and how
he has had mercy on you." So the man went away and
began to tell in the Decapolis how much Jesus had done
for him. And all the people were amazed.

—MARK 5:6-20

When Mark mentions the *Decapolis,* he is referring to a

group of ten cities. Those cities, like the man's home town, were filled with people who had not heard of Jesus. The people were amazed at his story. He had the scars to prove that his story was true. This man was eager to share his story with everyone. He had a new purpose and a new outlook on life.

It's likely that this man's story planted seeds of Jesus' message throughout Greek territory that would later be watered by Jesus' own trip to the Decapolis (Mark 7). In a way, the man was a missionary. That's a big leap from a demon possession!

Radical Change

I would like to share a little bit of my own story with you now. I do this in hope of illuminating a major message within the story of the Gerasene demoniac: God has the power to change lives. For the Gerasene demoniac, he took someone who had been living a meaningless life and gave him a purposed and refreshed outlook on life.

I tried marijuana for the first time when I was thirteen years old. It was fun and seemed fairly innocent. Soon, it became an everyday habit that I continually had to hide from my parents and others. I had a mild learning disability as a child and didn't feel that I fit in with the other kids in elementary school. I was one of the "special" kids. Other kids who received special attention because of a learning disability did all right, but I had trouble fitting in and was socially awkward. In middle school, weed gave me a sense of identity among some of my peers.

After about a year of using, my friends and I were arrested at a park for possession of marijuana.

During the six months between my arrest and court date, I began getting into harder drugs. I experimented with LSD. My friend and I heard about a certain brand of over-the-counter pills that could cause a trip, so we shoplifted a box. There were sixteen pills in the box, so we each took eight. The pills made our legs go numb, giving us the sense that we were floating when we walked. We later took ten each, which made everything in our vision double. The next time we took twelve each and experienced increasing effects, then fourteen, then a whole box of sixteen on two occasions.

Taking sixteen of those pills caused me to be completely out of touch and unaware. It wasn't anything that even sounds cool like being in another universe (which a drug trip like that really wouldn't be, either). It was a lessened, watered-down version of this world. The drug just made me temporarily stupid with hallucinations thrown in. I thought I was places that I really wasn't, I thought people were there who really weren't, and I felt like I was floating from one end of the room to the other. I remember thinking that I was going to die.

Prior to that time, I had thought such a trip would be great, but there is nothing great about losing all self-awareness and nearly dying in your early teens. I oftentimes describe myself during that time as existing and not truly living.

After six months, I went to court, was put on probation, and was required to meet with a drug counselor three times a week. God's grace worked through the counseling to provide me with some perspective, which helped lead me out of the stronger drugs. In the months that followed, I still grappled with marijuana and I found a way to beat the random drug tests I was required to take.

Every day was a battle between will and habit. Marijuana had become an addiction. I didn't even like using it anymore, but I did it anyway. The high feeling had become less about laughing and having the munchies and more about fear and paranoia. The music I listened to reinforced my miserable habit of still using drugs in spite of hating them.

After six months of using and lying to everyone, I was arrested for a second time the day before I was supposed to be let off probation. They didn't end my term of probation, and for the following six months I stayed clean because I was tired of being in trouble, feeling watched, covering up drug tests, and random police visits to search my room.

A lot of people say that if it weren't for parents, kids would never get into drugs, but if it weren't for mine, I would have never stopped. They are devoted Christians and wanted me to be as well. Throughout my whole struggle with drug use, I attended youth group functions at church. The youth minister, other leaders, and teens from the youth group would regularly reach out and invite me to events, retreats, and camps. I would say that I didn't want to go, and sometimes I really didn't, but a lot of times I enjoyed going. I liked going to these events because they gave me hope. It was encouraging to watch people my age enjoy true friendship that didn't revolve around something as shallow as drugs. They didn't have to constantly prove themselves to be anything more than who they really were. The friendship and community they had was genuine.

Six months after my second arrest, I was at a week-long church camp at the end of July. I was scheduled to be let off of probation on August 1st, so during that camp I was on the brink of deciding what direction my future would take. Would I stay clean and get involved with the church or start using drugs again? The teens and leaders at the camp were supportive of me and encouraged me not to return to drug use. When I got home, I was let off probation, and quickly began smoking weed again with the same friends I had before. I had returned to my default mode.

I smoked just as heavily as I had before. One summer day, we had been smoking quite a bit inside a friend's house. After we were all stoned, someone had the idea to go shoot baskets in the driveway. I didn't see the appeal of playing basketball while high, but I went anyway. When I stepped outside, the bright light of the day contrasted sharply with the dark room we had been in. It seemed as if I was temporarily blinded. I couldn't see and my body felt like it was doing back-flips. This blinded moment was a reflection of what my whole life was during that time— very little purpose and very little sense of direction.

I was able to feel my way back inside, where I sat down and prayed. It was one of those desperate prayers. I asked God for help and I felt my body come back into a more peaceful state. I didn't keep my end of the bargain I had made with God, though, as later that night I used again.

I kept smoking until December of that year. After Christmas, I attended a winter youth rally with the church. All the friends I had gotten to know from the youth group were there, and once again, I observed their authenticity toward one another and toward God. I had decided I didn't want drugs to be part of my future. I had had enough. I had gained enough self-confidence to make a major life change. I made a decision there that the way I had been living for three years wasn't fair to me, to my family, or to God. I knew that I was never going to use again. I didn't tell anyone about this conviction, because they had heard it before, but I knew it was real this time.

I never smoked weed or used any other drug again. I jumped head-first into involvement with the church and youth group, helping in whatever ways I could. My drug counselor had told me that most people experience a relapse after two-and-a-half to three months, but I never did. I credit that to God's strengthening power, and His use of a supporting Christian community. Being involved at a church that was actually doing good things gave me a true purpose and added real meaning to my life. I was able to play a little role in the big things that God was doing in the world.

From Death to Life

In his book *The Air I Breathe*, Loui Giglio writes, "God is always bringing the dead back to life and giving the lost unending purpose."[1] We can see that in the life of the Gerasene demoniac. The man who people thought would never contribute anything positive to society became the first Christian missionary. The man who had lived among the dead amazed people by telling them about his new life. The man who had attacked people at the tombs traveled from town to town and told people about God's power to heal. Living for Christ gave him a new purpose and direction, even though he had seemed beyond help. He went from being demon-possessed to being a missionary.

You may know someone or be someone that everyone thinks will never make a positive change. You may have faced so much trouble in your life that you don't think you have the power or ability to make a positive change. The Gerasene demoniac didn't have the power to change, either. He was trapped by the forces of evil that controlled his life. It was God's power that changed him, not his own. Have you ever invited God to work in your own life?

Points for Reflection/Discussion

➢ The man formerly known as the Gerasene Demoniac was made new by God. Have you ever felt or wanted to feel what it was like to be made new by God?

➢ Read Mark 5:18-20. Jesus gave the man a purpose and the man acted on it. Why is it important to have a purpose? What do you feel may be God's purpose for your life? Is God calling you to do something?

➢ We commonly hear people say, "Some people will never change." How does the story of the Gerasene demoniac prove that to be untrue?

➢ For the Gerasene demoniac, following God meant going from town to town and sharing about his experience with Jesus. What does following God mean for you?

Chapter Twelve

A Woman Arrested for Adultery:
Public Humiliation and a Fresh Start

"For God did not send his Son into the world to condemn the world, but to save the world through him." – John 3:17

THINK ABOUT A TIME WHEN you were embarrassed by your own actions. Imagine being caught in the middle of your most humiliating and sinful action and then imagine being taken to a public place for everyone to hear about it.

That's the beginning of the story of a woman who met Jesus one day. She was not planning on meeting Jesus, but the trouble she was in led her to Him. People have been meeting God through unusual circumstances for all of history, and this woman's story is one of those in which someone met God in the middle of a giant mess. The woman probably thought Jesus would condemn her, but He showed her and everyone else present what grace is all about.

The woman was in custody because she had been caught committing adultery, which was a crime in her culture. Her trial was a public and embarrassing one—she was taken to the church where people had gathered to hear Jesus teach early in the morning. They were surprised when she arrived with her prosecutors.

Since she was taken to the temple at dawn, it's likely that her affair had been discovered in the middle of the night. She may have been terrified and running on fear-fed adrenaline or the whole thing may have seemed tragically surreal.

Her reputation was ruined. Since she was Jewish, most of the people at the temple would probably know her or at least recognize her. The punishment for her actions was death. The only thing that could have outweighed the embarrassment and shame of her uncovered sin would have been the fear of her imminent execution.

The method of execution for her crime was stoning, in which people would throw rocks at an offender until the person died. Sometimes this happened at the city gate, but sometimes a woman who had been convicted of a sexual crime would be executed right in front of her parents' home (Deuteronomy 22:20-24). Based on what we know about her circumstance, this woman probably would have been executed at the city gate.

When I was a teenager, an organization that educates people about drunk driving visited my high school. We all went to the parking lot where they had placed a car that an intoxicated driver had crashed. It looked like a soda can that someone had stepped on. They wanted us to see the results of driving drunk.

When the people dragged the woman into the temple courts, everyone probably looked at her in the same way we had looked at the wrecked car. She was a tragedy on display for everyone to stare at. Her private affair had become a public matter:

> At dawn he [Jesus] appeared again in the temple courts, where all the people gathered around him, and he sat down to teach them. The teachers of the law and the Pharisees brought in a woman caught in adultery. They made her stand before the group and said to Jesus, "Teacher, this woman was caught in the act of adultery. In the Law, Moses commanded us to stone such women. Now what do you say?" They were using this question as a trap, in order to have a basis for accusing him.
>
> But Jesus bent down and started to write on the ground with his finger. When they kept on questioning him, he straightened up and said to them, "If any one of you is without sin, let him be the first to throw a stone at her." Again he stooped down and wrote in the ground.
>
> At this, those who heard began to go away one at a time, the older ones first, until only Jesus was left, with the woman still standing there. Jesus straightened up and asked her, "Woman, where are they? Has no one condemned you?"
>
> "No one, sir," she said.
>
> "Then neither do I condemn you," Jesus declared. "Go now and leave your life of sin."
>
> —JOHN 8:2-11

What do we Know About the Woman?

The woman had committed adultery, so was she married? She was probably engaged. The Pharisees mention in John 8:5 that the Old Testament taught that a woman who committed her crime should be stoned. The Old Testament law specifically describes stoning as the punishment for an *engaged* woman who committed adultery (Deuteronomy 22:20-21, 23-24).

For a married woman who committed adultery, however, the punishment was death by an unspecified method (Leviticus 20:10, Deuteronomy 22:22). Since the Pharisees stated that the Old Testament taught that the woman should be stoned, then we can safely assume she was engaged. Since she was engaged, she may have been fairly young—probably in her late teens or early twenties. Her relationship with her fiancé and extended family was most likely destroyed by her actions.

What Everyone There Had in Common with the Woman

In His response to the questions, Jesus showed that all people, whether they're publicly condemned or not, are in need of grace. They lived in a shame-and-honor culture, in which only the publicly condemned were put to shame. People with hidden sins were in good standing.

Jesus disrupted that way of thinking by challenging everyone to think about what they had in common with the woman instead of how they were different: "If any one of you is without sin, let him be the first to throw a stone at her" (John 8:5). Before Jesus said that, many people in the crowd had probably been dissecting her with judgmental stares from a comfortable distance, as if they were watching an episode of COPS. But Jesus pointed out that sin was the common denominator between the woman and everyone else there.

Grace

When everyone left and the woman told Jesus that nobody had condemned her, he responded, "Then neither do I condemn you." One author highlights an important insight here: "It is important to notice that Jesus did not say he did not find her guilty. She was guilty; he said he did not condemn her."[1] Adultery is a serious mistake with serious consequences (see Proverbs 5:1-23, 6:32, Matthew 5:27-30, and Hebrews 13:4). It's selfish, it betrays trust, and at its worst can break families apart and damage the psyche of a couple's child. This makes the message of Jesus more powerful: "I don't condemn you either." But if we just picture Jesus saying, "Not guilty," we will miss the best part of the story. He was extending grace.

Grace was a new concept at that time. The people were familiar with mercy, but mercy and grace are not exactly the same. It is often said that they are like opposite sides of the same coin. A person can be in need of mercy even if they have not done anything wrong. A medical mission team may travel to an impoverished part of the world in order to show mercy to people who are malnourished. Many living in extreme poverty did not bring their circumstances on themselves, but they are still in need of mercy. A blind man once asked Jesus to have mercy on him, even though it obviously wasn't his fault that he was blind (Luke 18:35-43). But people are in need of *grace* when they have messed up. Jesus knew the woman was guilty, and he gave her the opportunity to move forward and change her life.

A friend of mine was recently talking about the first time she signed up for *Facebook*. She said she went to *facebook.com* and it said, *Facebook: It's free and always will be*. She pointed out that that's how grace is.

God's grace is free and always will be. The only cost of grace is accepting it. Like any other gift, it can be refused, discarded, or forgotten. Truly accepting a gift means that we find a place for it in our lives. People refuse grace by pushing God away or forgetting about the grace they've received. They keep living on their own terms as if God doesn't exist.

Moving Forward

When everyone left, the woman was probably the most surprised of anyone that she had not been condemned. She had just been in crisis mode since she thought she was going to die. Up until that moment, she did not think she had a future. Even if she did make it out alive, her reputation was in ruins which was even a bigger deal then than it is now. Jesus, then, gave her a challenge for her future, "Go now and leave your life of sin" (John 8:11). Jesus implies that her life is worth continuing to live by challenging her to live a better, more responsible life going forward. Despite the wreckage she was in, the best days of her life may have been ahead of her – because of grace.

Points for Reflection/Discussion

➤ Jesus challenged the woman to move forward with her life despite what she had lost (reputation, probably a relationship, etc.) In what ways may God be challenging you to move forward despite what you have lost?

➤ The woman experienced deep shame when her affair was exposed to the crowd at the temple. Have you ever felt deeply humiliated?

➤ Why do you think Jesus didn't condemn the woman?

➤ In John 3:17, Jesus says, "For God did not send his Son into the world to condemn the world, but to save the world through him." What does this verse teach us about the nature of God?

➤ The Pharisees used the woman to try and trap Jesus. Have you ever felt used?

➤ What role does God's grace play in your life?

Chapter Thirteen

Jesus:
God Experienced What We Experience

*"Jesus was considered to be a criminal... I
identify with him on some parts, because he was
condemned..."* – Bobby Wallace, Inmate[1]

I RECENTLY WENT TO SAN Diego for a conference. The guy who
drove the hotel shuttle to the airport on the day I was leaving
asked me about my trip there. I told him I was in town for a
church leadership conference, and that I work for a church. He
said, "Oh, I didn't know you work for a church." He went on to say,
"Well, I have a lot of deep theological questions." I responded, "I
don't have a lot of deep theological answers."

On the way to the airport, he stopped at the zoo and a family
climbed out of the van. As we were driving from the zoo to the
airport, I brought the topic up again: "So you said you have some
questions about God." He pointed out the window and said, "Just

look around. It's obvious there's a creator." We were driving through a beautiful part of San Diego. He went on, "But to me, God is too big for one religion."

His statement challenged me to think about why I believe the story of Jesus as truth that we should all follow. As we were pulling into the airport, I said, "Let me take just a minute to explain why, for me, it has to be Jesus." He was open to that and told me to go ahead.

I hadn't really thought before about what I'd say to someone who believed in God but not in Jesus Christ, but I told him, "For me, it has to be Jesus because He is the only God who became human and experienced the things that I've experienced." I spent a couple of minutes talking about God's attempts in the Old Testament to be in a relationship with His people and how the Old Testament prophets spoke about the messiah (Jesus) that would come (as in Isaiah 53). Then we talked about Jesus' ministry in the New Testament. The guy was open to what I was saying. I recommended that he read the gospel of John, since belief and unbelief is a major theme in that book. As I was walking into the airport he called out to me and said that he was going to read it that day.

Jesus is the only God who became human and experienced what we experience. He was not part human and part God, He was fully human and fully God. The writer of Hebrews explains it:

> Since the children have flesh and blood, he too shared
> in their humanity so that by his death he might
> destroy him who holds the power of death—that is, the
> devil—and free those who all their lives were held in
> slavery by their fear of death.... For this reason, he had
> to be made like his brothers in every way, in order that

he might become a merciful and faithful high priest in service to God, and that he might make atonement for the sins of the people. Because he himself suffered when he was tempted, he is able to help those who are being tempted.

—HEBREWS 2:14-15; 17-18

Jesus became fully human and went through the things we have to go through. He knows what it's like to be tempted (see Matthew 4:1-11). Sometimes I've thought of Jesus' temptation episode as if it were a fixed boxing match in which it was already decided that Satan would lose. It wasn't fixed, though. Jesus was actually tempted to do evil. The writer of Hebrews says Jesus *suffered* when He was tempted. Later, the writer of Hebrews says, "For we do not have a high priest that is unable to sympathize with our weaknesses, but we have one who has been tempted in every way, just as we are—yet was without sin" (Hebrews 4:15).

Jesus knows what it's like to be misunderstood. He knows what it's like to be arrested. He knows what it's like to be betrayed (Luke 22:1-6). He knows how it feels to be made fun of (Luke 23:35-36). He knows what it's like to experience the grief of losing a loved one. His friend and cousin, John the Baptist, was murdered. Some say, "Well, that didn't really bother Jesus because Jesus knew that John was in Heaven." But you or I could lose someone we're close to, know they're in Heaven, and still have to go through a grieving experience. Basic human emotions like grief were part of the package of becoming human for Jesus in order to make atonement for us.

People in the Old Testament would offer animals as an atonement sacrifice to God. When Jesus came and was executed,

He was the atonement sacrifice that put an end to all other atonement sacrifices. Jesus became human, set an example for us, and paid for our atonement.

If Jesus had not become human, I would not be able to relate to Him. But since He has, we can look at the things He went through and identify common experiences. The Hebrews writer says that because Jesus experienced the things we experience, like temptation, He is able to help us through those things (2:18).

Through His arrest and crucifixion, it's as if Jesus jumped on a grenade that was packed with our sins—killing him and blowing our sin to pieces at the same time. He conquered death and made us clean before God.

Jesus' Arrest

Luke tells the story of Jesus' arrest:

While he was still speaking, a crowd came up, and the man who was called Judas, one of the Twelve, was leading them. He approached Jesus to kiss him, but Jesus asked him, "Judas, are you betraying the Son of Man with a kiss?"

When Jesus' followers saw what was going to happen, they said, "Lord, should we strike with our swords?" And one of them struck the servant of the high priest, cutting off his right ear.

But Jesus answered, "No more of this!" And he touched the man's ear and healed him.

Then Jesus said to the chief priests, the officers and the

temple guard, and the elders, who had come for him, "Am I leading a rebellion, that you have to come with swords and clubs? Every day I was with you in the temple courts, and you did not lay a hand on me. But this is your hour—when darkness reigns."

—LUKE 22:47-53

In the next two chapters, we will discuss some of the events that occurred after Jesus' arrest and during his trial and execution.

Points for Reflection/Discussion

➢ Read Philippians 2:1-11. What did Jesus surrender in order to come to earth? What was his attitude like when he was here?

➢ What does it mean to you that Jesus traded Heaven for a cross on earth? (Philippians 2:1-11)

➢ Read Matthew 26:47-56, Mark 14:43-52, Luke 22:47-53, and John 18:1-11. Jesus' arrest included elements of violence, strong emotion, betrayal, ambush, and abandonment. Have you ever given a lot of thought to the fact that Jesus was arrested?

➢ Matthew says that after Jesus' arrest, "All the disciples deserted him and fled." Have you ever felt deserted?

➢ What is the significance of Jesus' arrest (Luke 22:47-53), crucifixion (Luke 23:26-49), and resurrection (Luke 24) in your life?

Chapter Fourteen

Barabbas:
Set Free

BARABBAS WAS A REVOLUTIONARY WHO committed murder as part of an uprising against the Roman government in Jerusalem (Luke 23:19). He was arrested and was in prison at the same time that Jesus was on trial.

A crowd of Jews had gathered for Jesus' trial. They wanted Jesus to be sentenced to death. The Roman governor, Pilate, didn't want to execute Jesus. He recognized Jesus' innocence and his wife had been suffering from dreams about Jesus and advised Pilate not to be involved (Matthew 27:19). Pilate explained that each year the Roman government would release a Jewish prisoner from custody. The Jews got to choose who would be released. Pilate hoped the Jewish people would choose Jesus, but they chose Barabbas instead:

Pilate called together the chief priests, the rulers and the people, and said to them, "You brought me this man as one who was inciting the people to rebellion. I have examined him in your presence and found no basis for your charges against him.... Therefore, I will punish him and release him."

With one voice they cried out , "Away with this man! Release Barabbas to us!" (Barabbas had been thrown into prison for an insurrection in the city, and for murder.)

Wanting to release Jesus, Pilate appealed to them again. But they kept shouting, "Crucify him! Crucify him!"

For the third time he spoke to them: "Why? What crime has this man committed? I have found no grounds for the death penalty. Therefore I will have him punished and then release him."

But with loud shouts they insistently demanded that he be crucified, and their shouts prevailed. So Pilate decided to grant their demand. He released the man who had been thrown into prison for insurrection and murder, the one they asked for, and surrendered Jesus to their will.

—LUKE 23:13-25

It's likely that Barabbas's punishment, had it not been for Jesus, would have been crucifixion. The Romans crucified people that they wanted to make examples of in order to discourage the type of crime they were convicted of. An anti-Roman insurrectionist, who had murdered a Roman as part of a revolt, would definitely fit that category. Instead of being crucified, he went free so that Jesus could be crucified. Peter, speaking later to a group of Jews after Jesus' resurrection, said, "You disowned the Righteous and Holy One and asked that a murderer be released to you" (Acts 3:14).

Barabbas's story is symbolic for all of us because we all were set free from sin because of Jesus' death and resurrection. Hebrews 10:10 says, "...We have been made holy through the sacrifice of the body of Jesus once for all." Jesus laid his life down, and through that sacrifice He granted us life. It's as if we stepped on a land mine, and Jesus came and put his foot there, so we could walk off. That's the type of grace Jesus offers.

Points for Reflection/Discussion

➢ Read Ephesians 2:1-10. What does this passage teach about our sin and God's grace offered through Jesus?

➢ Colossians 2:13 says, "When you were dead in your sins...God made you alive with Christ. He forgave us all our sins, having cancelled the written code, with its regulations, that was against us and stood opposed to us; he took it away, nailing it to the cross." How does it feel to know that God forgives sins?

➢ Jesus was sentenced to death and Barabbas was released. In what ways is that story symbolic of the sacrifice Jesus made for you?

➢ Romans 6:3-4 says, "Or don't you know that all of us who were baptized into Christ Jesus were baptized into his death? We were therefore buried with him through baptism into death in order that, just as Christ was raised from the dead through the glory of the Father, we too may live a new life." Have you ever studied baptism or thought about being baptized? There are more passages about baptism in the next chapter.

➢ Read Isaiah 53. What do you learn about Jesus in that passage?

Chapter Fifteen

The Criminal on the Cross:
Death Row and Eternal Life

WHEN JESUS WAS DYING ON the cross, there were two criminals being crucified on either side of him. One mocked Jesus, but the other had a meaningful conversation with him. Their interaction led to the man finding grace and assurance of eternal life in the midst of his physical death:

> One of the criminals who hung there hurled insults at him: "Aren't you the Christ? Save yourself and us!"

> But the other criminal rebuked him. "Don't you fear God," he said, "since you are under the same sentence? We are punished justly, for we are getting what our deeds deserve. But this man has done nothing wrong."

Then he said, "Jesus, remember me when you come into your kingdom."

Jesus answered him, "I tell you the truth, today you will be with me in paradise."

—LUKE 23:39-43

The men on the cross next to Jesus are oftentimes referred to as thieves, but the word that the Bible uses to refer to them means *criminal* or *evil-doer*. Some speculate that they had been convicted of murder or part of a revolt against Rome, like Barabbas was. We can't know for certain what crimes they committed.

Crucifixion was a terrible way to die. In the midst of agonizing pain, the actual death was prolonged for hours and sometimes days. The word *excruciating* actually comes from the word crucifixion. Tony Ash, a biblical scholar, describes what Jesus and the two criminals endured on the cross (although Jesus had extra pain inflicted on Him during His crucifixion):

> Associated with crucifixions were great pain, difficulty in breathing and speaking, headaches, inability to keep the insects away, insults, and exposure to the elements. Death was slow and agonizing. A victim could hang several days before dying, raving mad.[1]

Another scholar adds that the person being crucified would slowly suffocate because fatigue would set in and they could not straighten up to fill their lungs with air.[2]

Eternal Life

God has the power to give you hope even if you are on death row. Even though it would have been physically difficult for Him to speak, Jesus told the man on the cross next to Him that "today you will be with me in paradise." The word Jesus used there for *paradise* was the word used to describe the Garden of Eden in the Old Testament (see Genesis 2-3). Even though they were experiencing the worst physical suffering imaginable, Jesus describes the place they will be as a peaceful and pleasurable area where God and people are together and happy. It is the same word used in Revelation 2:7: "To him who overcomes, I will give the right to eat from the tree of life, which is in the paradise of God."

If you are on death row, it may be too late for some things in life. There are some liberties you may never have again. You may feel like all of your second chances are gone. That was the reality for the criminal on the cross. When it's too late for other things, though, it's not too late to cultivate a meaningful relationship with God. It's not too late to develop confidence and understanding about your place in Heaven. *For more passages about Heaven, see the points for reflection and discussion at the end of this chapter.*

The man recognized that eternal life was not automatic. He reached out to Jesus in order to be assured of it. Accepting God's power in your life is not a passive activity. It involves change and spiritual growth. In Colossians 3:5-10, Paul discusses what practical steps a follower of Jesus should take toward change and spiritual growth.

Baptism

The criminal died with Jesus and was raised to new life, which is symbolic of what the New Testament teaches about being baptized into Christ. Paul says, "We were therefore buried with him through baptism into death in order that, just as Christ was raised from the dead through the glory of the father, we too may live a new life" (Romans 6:4). The New Testament teaches that we are saved through baptism (Mark 16:16, 1 Peter 3:21). When Jesus was baptized (Matthew 3:13-17), God's Holy Spirit descended on Him. For more passages about baptism, see the *points for reflection and discussion* at the end of this chapter.

Other Lessons

There are three other lessons in the man's story that we can apply to our own situations. First, he recognized that he was in need of grace. He said, "We are getting what our deeds deserve." Likewise, we are all in need of grace (see Titus 3:3-7).

Second, notice that the man on the cross had a personal interaction with Jesus. Scholars point out that this is one of few times when someone called Jesus by his name when talking to Him.[3] Usually they called him *teacher, rabbi,* or *Lord.* The criminal's interaction with Jesus was a close, intimate one. Your interaction with Jesus should be a close, intimate one, too. You should pray to Jesus about the things that are closest to your heart.

Finally, although he was dying, the rest of the man's earthly life from his encounter with Jesus onward was not wasted. The crowd heard the conversation between the man and Jesus, and it's possible that the man's loved ones may have been there and heard them talking. The story spread even further when the biblical writer Luke recorded the conversation. Countless people have heard or read the conversation and have been encouraged by it.

If you find Christ in prison or even on death row, this story offers hope. It teaches that not only does Jesus offer salvation, but also the chance to have an impact in the lives of others. There may be someone in your life that needs to know about the new hope you have found through Christ. 1 Peter 3:15 says to "always be prepared to give an answer to everyone who asks you to give the reason for the hope you have."

Conclusion

If you are on death row and your facility allows you to access music, I encourage you to listen to a song called *Thief* by a band called *Third Day*. It's a touching song written from the perspective of the criminal on the cross.[4]

Points for Reflection/Discussion

➤ What do you imagine Heaven is like?

➤ The Bible has several teachings about Heaven (Matthew 5:3, 10:32; John 3:16-17; Philippians 3:14, 3:20-21; Colossians 1:5; 1 Peter 1:4; Revelation 2:7). What do these passages teach you about Heaven?

➤ Read Philippians 1:20-26 and 2 Timothy 4:6-8. In what ways does Paul show confidence that after he dies, he will be with Jesus?

➤ Read Philippians 3:18-21. What contrasts does Paul draw between Heaven and earth?

➤ Read John 11:25-26. Do you believe what Jesus says there about eternal life?

➤ In the New Testament, baptism is prominently associated with a new life, forgiveness of sins, and receiving the Holy Spirit (for examples see Mark 16:16; Acts 2:38; Acts 8:36-38; Acts 9:18; Romans 6:4; Colossians 2:11-12; and

1 Peter 3:21). Jesus himself was baptized. Have you been baptized or ever considered being baptized?

➤ Who do you know that would be encouraged to hear about the faith and hope you have in Jesus?

Chapter Sixteen

Peter:
The Ministry of Angels in Prison

AFTER JESUS' DEATH AND RESURRECTION, Herod, an insecure and bloodthirsty governor, executed a Christian named James, who had been one of Jesus' disciples. The execution excited some of the non-Christian people, so Herod arrested Peter, another disciple of Jesus. He didn't have Peter executed right away, but he put him in prison and was planning to make a public display of his sentencing later on (see Acts 12:1-5).

Peter's friends were obviously concerned. After what had happened to James, they knew that Herod would kill Peter, too. While Peter was in jail, they got together at someone's house to pray for him. The night before his public trial and almost certain execution, an angel helped Peter:

> The night before Herod was to bring him to trial,

Peter was sleeping between two soldiers, bound with two chains, and sentries stood guard at the entrance. Suddenly an angel of the Lord appeared and a light shone in the cell. He struck Peter on the side and woke him up. "Quick, get up!" he said, and the chains fell off Peter's wrists...

Peter followed him out of the prison, but he had no idea that what the angel was doing was really happening; he thought he was seeing a vision. They passed the first and second guards and came to the iron gate leading to the city. It opened for them by itself, and they went through it. When they had walked the length of one street, suddenly the angel left him.

—Acts 12:6-7; 9-10

Peter stopped at the house where the group was praying for him, told them what happened, and then moved on.

Angels

You may be asking yourself whether there is any modern day application of Peter's escape story. It can be frustrating when we read stories in the Bible of angels saving people from inescapable situations. It's frustrating because many of us don't think about angels as a reality in our lives. Angels play a big role in the Bible, but a small one in most of our personal understandings of how God works today. Just because we don't think about them a lot, however, does not mean that angels aren't present in our lives.

We should keep in mind that angels are usually invisible. It's not that angels aren't real, it's that most of the time our vision doesn't allow us to see them. Even in the Bible, whenever a person sees an angel, it's noteworthy. We can't see them without God showing them to us, but even if God doesn't show us, they're no less real.

One of my professors in college worked as a missionary in Ghana for 26 years. Some of the people he ministered to were involved in dark magic. As a result, my friend saw many real, actual demons over the years that he was there. He told me that he had seen demons on multiple occasions, but had only seen an angel twice (the same one on two separate occasions). He explained that one major difference between angels and demons is that demons show themselves to intimidate and bully, while angels show themselves only when they need to be seen.

Angels are like bees. Bees help us by supporting the life of plants and crops, but we don't fully understand how. In the same way, angels are working all the time, but we don't see them and usually don't think about what they're doing.

In 2 Kings 6:15-17, Elisha and his servant were surrounded by their enemies on horses and chariots that were sent to capture them. The servant was terrified and asked Elisha, "Oh, my lord, what shall we do?" He thought they were about to be killed or captured. Elisha prayed that the servant's eyes would be opened and said, "Don't be afraid. Those who are with us are more powerful than those who are with them." At first, the servant may have wondered what Elisha meant. If I had been there, I would have thought that Elisha's words sounded cool but weren't very practical. But when God opened his eyes, he saw "the hills full of horses and chariots of fire...." The servant had not been able to see the godly forces that were there to fight for them until God revealed them to him.

Jesus taught that angels guard and help children. In Matthew 18:10, Jesus said, "Do not look down on one of these little ones.

For I tell you that their angels in heaven always see the face of my father in heaven." We know from several stories throughout Scripture that angels help adults, too. Hebrews 1:14 teaches that angels serve "those who will gain salvation." In Numbers 22:21-31, an unseen angel helps someone by blocking a path that would have led to harm.

The Ministry of Angels in Prison

I hadn't really thought a lot about angels until my close friend went to prison. I felt depressed and helpless. I felt a gripping despair that I couldn't shake off. Knowing someone in prison who you cannot help is hard. It's like having a cast on your arm and the skin underneath is always itching but you can't get to it. It feels like there's nothing you can do. I had never wanted so much to do something helpful but felt so powerless. I carried the burden of sadness around with me like a bucket of concrete hung around my neck.

I prayed that God would not only be with my friend, but that He would send an angel to comfort him and give him strength and encouragement. I didn't care that it sounded illogical. The situation was desperate—and, in the Bible, that is when angels often get involved. I had never thought a whole lot about angels before because I had never had such a concern for someone whom I felt powerless to help. Through this prayer, God provided me with assurance that He, in some way, was watching over and protecting my friend.

No Place is Off Limits to God

One takeaway from Peter's jail story is that prison is not off limits to God's work. The boundaries of God's love don't exist on earth. God's compassion is there whenever there is pain, loneliness, and regret. In Psalm 34:7, David says that "the angel of the Lord encamps around those who fear him, and he delivers them." In David's context, the word *fear* meant to respect and revere.

Of course, an angel is probably not going to break you out of prison as it did with Peter, but God can use them to provide protection and strength. As Hebrews 1:14 teaches, angels serve God's purposes. In John 3:16-17, Jesus teaches about this purpose:

> For God so loved the world that he gave his one and only Son, that whoever believes in him shall not perish but have eternal life. For God did not send his Son into the world to condemn the world, but to save it through him.

God wants to reconcile His people with Him through Jesus. Angels are part of God's supporting cast in that effort, and they are one of many tools that God uses to accomplish His purposes. He also uses people, the Holy Spirit, and all types of circumstances to show His love.

Points for Reflection/Discussion

➤ What do you believe about the work of angels today?

➤ Acts 12:5 tells us that when Peter was in prison, his friends prayed for him. Have you ever prayed for someone in prison or had anyone pray for you? If the answer is no, who do you know that would pray for you if asked? Who should you pray for?

➤ In Romans 8:38-39, Paul says that "I am convinced that neither death nor life, neither angels nor demons, neither the present nor the future, nor any powers, neither height nor depth, nor anything else in all creation, will be able to separate us from the love of God that is in Christ our Lord." How does it make you feel to know that prison cannot separate you from God's love?

➤ How do Jesus' words in the following passage make you feel? "For God did not send his Son into the world to condemn the world, but to save it through him" (John 3:17).

Chapter Seventeen

Paul:
Contentment in a Bad Situation

"Finding something redemptive about the suffering
we've experienced could be the beginning of healing."
– Donald Miller (on his Twitter account)

EARLY IN HIS LIFE, PAUL (known then as Saul) persecuted the church. In the time following Jesus' crucifixion and resurrection, he arrested Christians. He gave approval to the execution of a follower of Jesus named Stephen (Acts 8:1). He radically changed his life after Jesus appeared to him in a vision on the road (see Acts 9:1-22). After that, he was arrested multiple times for sharing the message of Jesus. During an incarceration late in his life, he wrote these words:

> ... I have learned to be content whatever the
> circumstances. I know what it is to be in need, and

> I know what it is to have plenty. I have learned the
> secret of being content in any and every situation,
> whether well fed or hungry, whether living in plenty
> or in want. I can do everything through him who gives
> me strength.

—PHILIPPIANS 4:11-13

Those are not words that we would expect to hear from someone who is in prison and doesn't really deserve to be, like Paul. Years earlier, Paul had been arrested with another Christian leader named Silas. After they were "severely flogged" (Acts 16:23), they were taken to jail. That night, God caused an earthquake which set forth a chain of events that led to their release the next day (Acts 16:25-36).

Years later (when he wrote those words to the Philippians), Paul was imprisoned again, but there was no sign of a miraculous escape. There were no earthquakes and no angels to break him out of prison. But Paul still had a good attitude. He was content. If it had been me, I would have probably started to have depressing thoughts like "maybe God just doesn't work the same way He did before" or "maybe I'm not as meaningful to God now as I was back then."

It's easy for us to suspect God doesn't care about us when He works differently in some situations than in others. But Paul didn't think that way. If we look at earlier parts of the same letter, we can see why:

> Now, I want you to know, brothers, that what has
> happened to me has really served to advance the gospel.
> As a result, it has become clear throughout the whole
> palace guard and to everyone else that I am in chains for
> Christ. Because of my chains, most of the brothers in the

Lord have been encouraged to speak the word of God more courageously and more fearlessly.

—PHILIPPIANS 1:12-14

Seeing godly value in a situation can help lead to contentment. That was Paul's secret. He chose to focus on the good his situation brought rather than on the limitations it presented. Were there other places he would have rather been? Yes. He told the church in Philippi that he longed to be with them (Philippians 1:8) and mentioned that he hoped to visit them soon (Philippians 2:24). Paul didn't say that he never felt the pressures of prison life or that he never felt disappointed, lonely, sorrowful, or upset. He said that he'd learned to be content.

We can get angry with God when He doesn't act the way we think He should. Paul had experienced God working in miraculous ways, but later he saw God at work in more subtle yet equally significant ways. Maybe you can see godly value in your situation even if you are imprisoned. There may be a big lesson that God is teaching you through your imprisonment that will make the rest of your life better than it would have been if you had never gone to prison. If we surrender to God, He is always able to use bad situations to bring about good ones. Even if we don't see value in our situation, Paul would say that we should look to Jesus for contentment.

I recently met a guy who had lost both of his legs in a car accident. He had been riding in the bed of a pickup truck when an eighteen-wheeler ran into it. The impact sent him flying out of the truck. Over the next nine months, he lost both of his legs to amputations.

Years later, after struggling through depression and alcoholism, he began competing in athletic events and went on to complete the Hawaiian ironman triathlon. This includes a 2.4-mile swim, a 112-mile bike ride, and 26.2 miles of running. When I heard him speak at a conference, he explained that he was able to see the good that came from his situation because losing his legs had opened many doors for him to share the way God had helped him.[1] I told him that his attitude about his legs reminded me of Paul's attitude about prison.

At many other points in his life, Paul faced difficulties and had to keep his focus on Christ in order to maintain a positive attitude. Without hope and power from God, he could not have persevered through all of the problems. In a letter to the church in Corinth, he described troubles he had faced in the form of imprisonment, violence, and other dangers:

> I have worked much harder, been in prison more frequently, been flogged more severely, and been exposed to death again and again. Five times I received from the Jews the forty lashes minus one. Three times I was beaten with rods, once I was stoned, three times I was shipwrecked, I spent a night and a day in the open sea, I have been constantly on the move. I have been in danger from rivers, in danger from bandits, in danger from my own countrymen, in danger from Gentiles; in danger in the city, in danger in the country, in danger at sea; and in danger from false brothers. I have labored and toiled and have often gone without sleep. I have known hunger and thirst and have often gone without food; I have been cold and naked. Besides everything else, I face daily the pressure of my concern for all the churches.
>
> —2 Corinthians 11:23-28

Paul was able to see godly value in his imprisonment and all of the other hardships he faced, which led to contentment. We're not always able to see the way God may be using a tough situation right away. Not everyone in the Bible was able to either (see Psalm 55:1-5 and Psalm 88). Sometimes we have to search for it and pray that God will find a way to be glorified through our painful circumstances.

Points for Reflection/Discussion

➤ God didn't work the same way during Paul's imprisonment that we read about in Philippians as He had with Paul's imprisonment in Acts 16. Have you ever felt like God has worked differently in one situation in your life than He did in another?

➤ Have you ever seen a bad situation that God was able to use for good?

➤ Why is it important to find contentment through our relationship with Christ?

➤ In the letter to the Philippians, Paul uses the word *rejoice* eight times. Even though he was in prison, he rejoiced and wanted others to as well. What has God done that makes you want to rejoice?

Conclusion

Jehoiachin:
Trading in Your Prison Clothes

JEHOIACHIN, A SINFUL KING OF Judah, was arrested at the age of 18 after another king invaded Jerusalem and took him as prisoner. He was in prison for 37 years, over twice the number of years he had been alive before his arrest. He entered prison in late adolescence and was released when he was a senior citizen. His prison life made up a lot of what he knew. This passage tells the story of his release after all of those years:

> In the thirty-seventh year of the exile of Jehoiachin king of Judah, in the year Evil-Merodach became king of Babylon, he released Jehoiachin from prison…. He spoke kindly to him and gave him a seat of honor higher than those of the other kings who were with him in Babylon. So Jehoiachin put aside his prison

clothes and for the rest of his life ate regularly at the king's table.

—2 Kings 25:27-29

The Bible does not say that Jehoiachin changed his lifestyle when he left prison, but there is still a valuable lesson in the story of his release. After 37 years in prison, he traded in his prison clothes for a new life. We don't know what Jehoiachin's prison experience consisted of, but we know that he was ready to trade it in by the time he was released. He'd had enough.

If we think of Jehoiachin's prison clothes as a metaphor, it can challenge us to think about what attribute we may want to trade in when we leave prison. When and if you are released from prison, you can trade in something old (like Jehoiachin did with his prison clothes) for a new life. Is there an ungodly trait that you want to trade in as you move forward with your life? What Christ-like characteristic do you want to trade it in for?

Every one of us, incarcerated or not, has something we should let go of in order to be more Christ-like. My mother-in-law recently told me about a show she saw called *Closet Intervention*. It was about people who hoarded and stockpiled tons of clothes and would never get rid of them. The producers of the show found that when the hoarders got rid of 75% of their clothes, they actually felt like they had more clothes. In the same way, if we give away our ungodly attributes that we have a tendency to hold on to, we will feel like we can get more out of life and we will have enriched relationships with God and others.

In 2 Corinthians 5:17, Paul says, "Therefore, if anyone is in Christ, he is a new creation; the old has gone, the new has come!" So what will you trade in? Bitterness? Hostility? Anger? Jesus says, "Love your enemies and pray for those who persecute you.... If you love only those who love you, what reward will you get?" (Matthew 5:44, 46).

Will you trade in revenge? Paul teaches in Romans 12:19-20 that revenge belongs to God. Paul then says, "Do not be overcome by evil, but overcome evil with good" (Romans 12:21).

Will you trade in old habits? Part of getting rid of old habits is making new, healthier habits. Remember that Daniel made it a habit of praying every day no matter what.

You may need to trade in impure thoughts. Paul says, "Whatever is true, whatever is noble, whatever is right, whatever is pure, whatever is lovely, whatever is admirable—if anything is excellent or praiseworthy—think about such things" (Philippians 4:8).

You may need to trade in self-focus for self-awareness. God spoke to the people through the prophet Haggai and said, "Give careful thought to your ways" (Haggai 1:5). If we are too self-focused, our actions will affect other people and we may not even realize it.

You may want to trade in an addiction, which of course can be difficult. It would be good to meet with a counselor if you need help working through some things. We all need counseling from time to time, even if it's just to get through a tough situation. Many churches offer it for free.

When thinking about what you will trade in when you leave prison, it may be helpful to try to identify and reflect on the core issue that led to the trouble you found yourself in. Many times, someone's criminal behavior is a result of a deeper issue. If we can't identify and address that main issue, we will have a hard time avoiding the behavior it leads to. Some ways to identify and address that main issue are: self-reflection, meeting with a counselor or therapist, or having a discussion with a pastor or mentor and getting advice from them about next steps.

The actions I mentioned above will require a lot honesty and vulnerability. But many people return to prison after they're released because they return to their previous lifestyle. Following through on those suggestions will make it less likely for you to return to prison.

Godly and Ungodly Characteristics

Paul shared the passage below to help believers in Galatia identify ungodly characteristics in their own lives. He contrasted those ungodly characteristics with the fruit of the Spirit. When thinking about the challenge of what you would like to trade in, it will be helpful to find something from his first list (the acts of sinful nature) that you would like to trade in for something from the second list (the fruit of the Spirit).

> The acts of the sinful nature are obvious: sexual immorality, impurity and debauchery; idolatry and witchcraft; hatred, discord, jealousy, fits of rage, selfish ambition, dissensions, factions and envy; drunkenness, orgies, and the like. I warn you, as I did before, that those who live like this will not inherit the kingdom of God.

> But the fruit of the Spirit is love, joy, peace, patience, kindness, goodness, faithfulness, gentleness and self-control. Against such things there is no law. Those who belong to Jesus Christ have crucified the sinful nature with its passions and desires.

> —GALATIANS 5:16-24

What attribute(s) that Paul mentions in the first list above (the acts of the sinful nature), would you like to trade in for something from the fruit of the Spirit list? Which fruit(s) of the Spirit would you like to allow God to develop more in your life?

_____

_____

_____

_____

_____

Even if we feel that we don't naturally have the fruit of the Spirit that Paul lists, it's important to remember that it comes from God, not ourselves. If we pray for it, God will give it to us. It comes from living by the Spirit.

Trading

Below is an acrostic that may be helpful when you, like Jehoiachin, are ready to set aside parts of your past and trade them in for something better:

Turning to God (2 Chronicles 33:12-13)

Reflecting on past behavior (Ephesians 2:1-10)

Accepting guidance and wisdom from others (Proverbs 10:17, 15:5, 15:32)

Developing spiritual discipline (Daniel 6:10)

Imitating Christ (Ephesians 5:1)

Navigating through challenges and obstacles in a godly way (Isaiah 42:16)

Giving back and helping others (Matthew 25:34-45)

Each of the lines above shouldn't be looked at as steps to be completed, but rather as parts of our commitment to God to which we continually devote ourselves.

Points for Reflection/Discussion

➢ What attribute might God be calling you to trade in?

➢ What godly attribute do you have that you would like to develop more?

➢ Read Ephesians 6:13-18. What godly piece of armor described there is the most appealing to you?

Recommended Reading

Hurting with God:
Learning to Lament with the Psalms

by Glenn Pemberton

When facing times of sorrow or anger, our tendency may be to not read the Bible. Pemberton's book shows how the Bible can be an outlet for expressing our sadness and disappointment with God. When discussing his book, Pemberton said "The lament Psalms give a voice to those who are holding onto faith by their fingernails."

Published by Leafwood Press.

Grace Gifts:
Discovering the Unique Joy God Has For You

by Dan Knight

God has gifted you with certain talents and abilities. You may have heard this referred to before as *spiritual giftedness*. God wants you to use the gifts He has given you to do something significant. Knight's book helps you determine what your gifts from God are by using the inventory included in the book. Knight also makes suggestions about how you may use your gifts and describes how people in the Bible used the same gifts that you have.

Published by Westbow Press.

Living Jesus:
Doing What Jesus Says in the Sermon on the Mount

by Randy Harris

A practical and insightful look at how the teachings of Jesus should impact our lives.

Published by Leafwood Press.

A Million Miles in a Thousand Years:
What I Learned While Editing My Own Life

by Donald Miller

I would recommend this book to anyone I know. It's honest and inspiring. Miller describes what he learned about stories when someone approached him about making a movie based on his life. Miller challenges his readers to think about what type of story they're telling with their lives, and how to tell a better one. He discusses all the elements of a good story and how we can find these elements within the stories we are living. He tells his own story in bits and pieces throughout the book in a compelling way.

Published by Thomas Nelson

The Spiritual Discipline Handbook

by Adele Ahlberg Calhoun

Calhoun's book includes descriptions of over sixty spiritual disciplines. You don't need to read each chapter, but it's a great resource and will give you an in-depth look at the spiritual disciplines that you may find to be the most rewarding. It may give you ideas about how to be spiritually disciplined that you haven't thought of before.

Published by Inter-Varsity Press.

Before Stones Become Bread: Becoming More Like Jesus by Resisting Temptation

by Chris Seidman

This book equips its readers with tools needed to deal with temptation in a healthy, Christ-like way.

Published by HeartSpring Publishing.

Acknowledgements

I would like to thank the friends and family who offered help and encouragement while I was writing this book. Your interest and support helped fuel my desire to work on it. Thank you.

I'd also like to thank my wife, Rachel, for affirming the importance of this book and for letting me go away for days at a time to work on it. I missed you though—because you are really fun to hang out with.

About the Cover Artist

Loren O'Laughlin grew up in Sacramento and was pulled in every direction by the world despite being raised in a God-fearing family. When he was arrested for theft at 16, he took a long hard look at his life and committed himself to following Jesus' example. Loren graduated from Oklahoma Christian University with a Bachelor's of Fine Arts. He shares his faith and stories of God's mystery through his paintings. Loren often uses found materials and military surplus in his art as a metaphor for the way God uses us to do His will, not just in spite of our past, but because of it.

You can see more of his paintings at www.livepainters.com.

References

Joseph: The Difficulties of Prison Life

1. Theological Lexicon of the Old Testament. Ernst Jenni and Claus Westermann. Translated by Mark E. Biddle. Hendrickson Publishers. Peabody, Mass. 1997. Page 1323-1324.

2. Dietrich Bonhoeffer's Prison Poems. Editor and Translator: Edwin Robertson. Zondervan. 1999. Page 57.

3. From the essay Optimism by Helen Keller. Published by C.P. Crowell and Company in November of 1903.

How Joseph Handled Temptation

1. Chris Seidman, *Before Stones Become Bread: Becoming More Like Jesus by Resisting Temptation* (Joplin: HeartSpring Publishing, 2006), 31.

Moses: God Can Use Anyone

1. Acts 7:30

2. Professor Jerry Taylor shared this in his keynote address at the 2007 *Summit* Lectureship at Abilene Christian University.

3. To view Annie's video testimony on iamsecond.com, visit http://www.iamsecond.com/seconds/annie-lobert/.

Daniel: Spiritual Discipline in Captivity

1. Goldingay, John, *Daniel* (Word Biblical Commentary 30; Nashville: Nelson Reference & Electronic, 1989).

Shadrach, Meshach, and Abednego: Real Trust in God

1. C.S. Lewis, *The Screwtape Letters* (New York: HarperOne, 1946), 15

2. Parade Magazine. October 16th, 2011 edition: http://www.parade.com/celebrity/sunday-with/2011/10/16-tim-allen-html

John the Baptist: Murdered in Prison

1. *New Interpreter's Bible Dictionary.* Volume 2. 806. Nashville: Abindgon Press. 2006.

2. Chambers, Oswald. *The Quotable Oswald Chambers.* Discovery House Publishers. Grand Rapids, MI. Compiled and edited by David McCasland. Quote from page 118.

The Gerasene Demoniac: God's Power to Change a Life

1. Louie Giglio, *The Air I Breathe: Worship as a Way of Life* (Sisters, Or.: Multnomah Publishers, Inc., 2003), 46.

A Woman Arrested for Adultery: Public Humiliation and a Fresh Start

1. Chris Bullard, *Cultural Windows Into the Gospel of John* (Kansas City: WOJI Press, 2002), 52.

Jesus: God Experienced What We Experience

1. This quote is from an article written by John Burnett of www.wbur.org on June 23, 2012. The article is about a Christian play performed by a group of inmates from a Louisiana State Penitentiary. Burnett interviewed Bobby Wallace, who played the role of Jesus in the play.

The Criminal on the Cross: Death Row and Eternal Life

1. Anthony Lee Ash, *The Gospel of Luke Part II* (Living Word Commentary Series 4; Austin: Sweet Publishing Company, 1973), 141.

2. Luke Timothy Johnson, *The Gospel of Luke* (Sacra Pagina Commentary 3; Collegeville: The Liturgical Press, 1991), 376.

3. Ibid 378.

4. Third Day. *Self-titled album,* track 6.Provident Music Distribution, 1996.

Paul: Contentment in a Bad Situation

1. If you would like to learn more about his story, you can read his book: *Unthinkable: The true Story about the First Double Amputee to Complete the World-Famous Hawaiian Ironman Triathlon.* By Scott Rigsby and Jenna Glatzer. Tyndale House Publishers. 2009.

CPSIA information can be obtained
at www.ICGtesting.com
Printed in the USA
FSHW011015060721
82991FS